"This book is so useful for (business journey, and it is w that enables the read comprehend the advice regardless of academic level or professional status. If you want to help others or are seeking help yourself, I highly recommend you read this, apply its lessons and use it to support others in a meaningful way."
– Julie Hawkins SMBN CIC

"Health and energy and an idea are all important things when you start a business but you need other things too, like knowledge about business, how to do things, where to get assistance, actually what to do and in what order. Starting Something with Nothing gives great no-nonsense advice with easy-to-read, straightforward common sense. Bob and Karen have years of real-life experience and you can benefit. It sets out all the basics in a sensible order and it really does show you how to get started with nothing. It's definitely worth reading."
– Steve Jones

STARTING SOMETHING WITH NOTHING

How to start in business no matter where you are today

Copyright © 2023 Bob Shepherd & Karen Davies

The moral right of the author has been asserted.

Apart from any fair dealing for the purposes of research or private study, or criticism or review, as permitted under Copyright, Design and Patents Act 1998, this publication may only be reproduced, stored or transmitted, in any form or by any means, with prior permission in writing of the publishers, or in any case of the reprographic reproduction in accordance with the terms of licences issued by the Copyright Licensing Agency. Enquiries concerning reproduction outside these terms should be sent to the publishers.

PublishU Ltd

www.PublishU.com

Scripture taken from the Holy Bible, New King James Version,
© 1982 by Thomas Nelson, Inc.
All rights reserved.

Scripture from the Holy Bible, New International Version®, NIV®.
Copyright © 1973, 1978, 1984, 2011 by Biblica, Inc.™ Used by permission of Zondervan. All rights reserved worldwide.

Scripture taken from the Holy Bible, New Living Translation,
copyright ©1996, 2004, 2007
by Tyndale House Foundation. Used by permission of Tyndale House Publishers, Inc.,
Carol Stream, IL 60188. All rights reserved.

All rights of this publication are reserved.

Thanks

The authors would like to thank the staff team at Purple Shoots who continue to support people to start something with nothing in the face of many frustrations.

Contents

Introduction

Chapter One	Who We Are
Chapter Two	Who We Help
Chapter Three	How We Do It
Chapter Four	The Senses of Business
Chapter Five	Watching the People
Chapter Six	Shouting to the Outside World
Chapter Seven	Listening to the Outside World
Chapter Eight	Watching the Money
Chapter Nine	The Bits You'd Rather not Touch
Chapter Ten	Following Your Nose
Chapter Eleven	Strategies for the Future
Appendix 1	Some Stories
Appendix 2	Cashflow Template

BOB SHEPHERD & KAREN DAVIES

Introduction

This book draws on our experience offering microfinance in Wales. It is to celebrate our success through the many small businesses that have been created with our funds by brave entrepreneurs and is also aimed at encouraging other amateur entrepreneurs to take that step and create a business of their own.

The bulk of the book is about how to start and run a micro-business – skip to those chapters if that is where your interest lies.

At the end, we tell some of the stories of people who have started businesses with a small loan from us.

BOB SHEPHERD & KAREN DAVIES

Chapter One
Who We Are

Purple Shoots is a registered charity and an ethical finance provider. We started in 2013 with the aim of providing small loans at ethical rates to people starting or running a business who couldn't get funding from anywhere else. It wasn't because we felt sorry for them or because we wanted to "help" but because in our careers we had seen many people with great potential as small entrepreneurs who were being wasted because they couldn't get their businesses started and we believed that communities and economies were poorer without them.

We take a different view from the established Finance Industry of providing finance to our customers. By treating each one individually (meeting and talking with everyone so that everyone has a chance to explain their business and their circumstances to us and we can make sure that we have understood everything), we gain insights unavailable to the normal lender. We don't use algorithms to make our lending decisions: there is no "computer says no." Instead, each application is decided on its own merits. Sometimes those merits outweigh the objections that would kill the proposition in the eyes of a mainstream finance company.

Ours is a simple, personal process (although we have been complimented on its thoroughness by numerous bodies). We do credit checks but a poor score doesn't necessarily rule someone out. To help our potential clients, we've tried to get rid of financial or business jargon so that no one is put off from coming to us to talk a business through. We offer support and advice both before and after a loan is made, often through volunteer entrepreneurs and people from the local business community who are keen to support what we do.

In our years of operation so far, we have met many awe-inspiring people who have sometimes overcome quite terrible things in their past or who have simply not given up in the face of setbacks and rejections by other providers. This book is all about those people. They are not down-and-outs; they are down but still fighting for consideration and a chance to stand up again.

STARTING SOMETHING WITH NOTHING

BOB SHEPHERD & KAREN DAVIES

Chapter Two
Who We Help

"Wasters," "Scroungers," "Lazy" and many more words like these are sadly what many people in the United Kingdom believe about people on Government benefits. Through our work, we can point at thousands of people to prove that this view is wrong.

There are many reasons that people find themselves in the benefits system and the spiral down into poverty as a result can be surprisingly fast.

If you are made redundant and you have a reasonable redundancy payout and some savings, you will find that you can't claim benefits until most of that money is spent. So whilst you're looking for a new job or developing an idea to start a business, your financial resources are steadily dwindling as you need them to live until, eventually, you are forced to claim benefits.

Back when you were working, you might have taken on a mortgage or finance for home improvements or a car. Without your income from your job, you will suddenly find it a struggle to pay these. It won't be long before "defaults" begin to appear on your credit score. The more there are, the lower your score will plummet, reducing your chances of raising any sort of finance to improve your circumstances to zero. A county court judgement (CCJ) will write you off for any consideration at all from mainstream lenders, leaving you at the mercy of the sharks or the questionable high interest lenders who accept that most of their lending will fail.

In addition, whilst benefits will provide the basics to live (although that is debatable – payments are frequently below what the government considers to be the minimum to keep people out of poverty), they don't provide enough for a crisis, such as a broken washing machine, transport costs for hospital visits etc. These are what force many people into the hands of the high-cost credit providers as they are the only financial institutions who will lend to people with poor credit scores and little income.

If you develop a serious long-term health condition, your employer may support you for a while, but if it persists, the chances are you will lose your job or be reduced to claiming sickness benefit. Either way, you'll be in the benefits system and all the issues outlined above will apply.

Most people in poverty weren't always poor and got there because something like the above two scenarios happened. Others struggle to get into the world of employment for a range of reasons: a disability, a caring responsibility, a life crisis that has left a lasting impact or simply because they can't find an outlet for the skills they have. As a result, they go from one temporary job to another temporary job (usually on very low pay) or are forced to rely on benefits.

This is dispiriting in the extreme and leads to depression, low confidence and isolation which then compounds the difficulty of finding work. If you are young with little experience and just starting out – even though you initially had plenty of enthusiasm – this is particularly hard to take.

People in all those circumstances are not people with no chance and no skill, but people with potential and ability who become trapped in a cycle of poverty which is difficult to break. They are written off by many organisations and institutions and have to put up with the negative attitudes of the wider public towards them. All these situations make it even harder for them to change things for the better – which is invariably what they want to do.

Purple Shoots was set up for people like this.

In our work for other financial institutions, we kept coming across people who were trying to build better lives for themselves and their families through starting their own independent business: effectively creating their own job which used the talents they recognised in themselves and seizing an opportunity which they could see in their community. Because they had no funds to put into a business themselves and no friends or family with any money either (and usually a poor credit score as a result of the struggle to live on benefits), the organisations we worked for would turn them down when they applied for finance to turn their plans into reality. This seemed to us to be a terrible waste of an entrepreneurial spirit and all the skills of the individual and was a lost potential contribution to the local economy.

BOB SHEPHERD & KAREN DAVIES

STARTING SOMETHING WITH NOTHING

BOB SHEPHERD & KAREN DAVIES

Chapter Three
How We Do It

Business is a lot of things and you can read large complicated text books about any particular aspect of it. At Purple Shoots we like simplicity and you can break down the requirements for business quite well without writing hundreds of pages of deep thought.

It might be useful to consider how we view an application for a loan. A mainstream lending company uses algorithms and standard formulae to judge the strength of a business idea, coupled with checks on who is involved. The principles are that the lending company is not going to run the business for you and once the loan is made, the money is in the hands of the borrower to carry out their plans. As such, they need to be sure of the borrower(s) and the business. Certain safeguards are put in place to try to secure repayment (charges on property, a personal guarantee), in case everything goes wrong. The greater the sum lent, the more checks and safeguards are put into place.

Clearly, for the people we've described who have found themselves excluded by these systems, they will for the most part, have fallen at the first hurdle. Purple Shoots has to look past all these requirements and find ways to justify assistance on another level. Fundamentally, it means we meet the person applying for a loan so we can talk through the business idea and the issues that are holding them back.

That isn't to say we ignore the principles of lending. We take note of credit searches for example. But we do not automatically reject an applicant who has accumulated a poor credit rating. There could be many reasons why that has occurred, and we look for an explanation.

An old training mnemonic for lending, "CAMPARI", still holds as good as any other. The answers are drawn from all the communications we receive (both verbal and written), plus independent information and checks where relevant.

The total assessment is based upon a balanced view of all these aspects. If anyone falls short, then we require some positive weighting in another to make up for it. We also consider what we know or could expect from a particular business idea. Does it make sense in the context in which they are to operate, with location, market, pricing, equipment and people involved?

C. Customer: Who is the applicant? What do we know of him/her/them? Where are they based and what history do we have or can we see? We are obliged under our licence to check identity and we obviously care that our applicant is being honest and straightforward with us. Inconsistencies shine out easily! In some cases it isn't so much what we're being told that matters, but what we aren't being told!

A. Ability: How is it that the applicant thinks they have the skills and attributes needed for this business idea? Does this fit with the likely requirements? Are there any personal qualities needed that the client needs or perhaps does not have? What experiences do they have that are likely to be useful? If training is reported how relevant is it? How does the applicant see the business idea themselves? Does their personality fit? A personal trainer with a shy or unattractive personality is going to struggle, for example.

M. Means: This is "means" in the old-fashioned sense. What does the client have to contribute to the business idea or what other income do they have (even if it's only benefits)? For example, do they have a vehicle that can be used? Do they have a partner that can support the household requirements while this business gets under way? We have seen many Business Plans (more on those later...) where there is no recognition that the business owner needs to eat and pay bills during the first few months whilst the business is getting off the ground.

P. Proposition: The business idea has to make sense. It has to be in proportion and the location needs to be right. There are often compromises but if that is the case then some action needs to be taken to compensate. We had an application for a café based in a small dormitory residential area. Most people left the area during the day to go to work, taking their café requirements with them.

We have had applications for shop premises. A shop needs stocking with goods and it takes a lot of money to make a shop look interesting. An empty shop is not attractive and if it's in a secondary location, in order to keep the costs down, we have two problems immediately.

A. Amount: Purple Shoots advances relatively small sums of money. Our average loan is around £2,700. That's perhaps enough to get a van or buy some equipment or finance a driving instructor's course. Business applications that have been turned down by the government's SULC scheme for, say £12,000, and that come to us for a much smaller sum invites an obvious question. What makes you think the business you had in mind that required £12,000 can make do with £3,000 and still get off the ground successfully? There may be an answer. If there an answer then the reverse applies Why did you apply for a much larger sum when you didn't actually need it?

R. Repayment: Purple Shoots charges interest but it's not enough to pay for "the doing" of the lending. The rest is subsidised by grants and donations to keep the process, our offices and other activities going. Our licence requires us to ensure that the repayment for any loan isn't going to cause hardship. In practice, our loans are very manageable and even if the business fails, the loan isn't so much that it should cause a big problem. We are flexible.

If any borrower gets into difficulties, we are there to help (it is in our interest to do so, after all) and we may reduce the repayment for a while or come to some other arrangement as well as helping with business ideas. We also check what the applicant's household requirements are beforehand. The best plan is for the business to be successful and afford the repayments easily. Most of our clients can do that.

Insurance: All our clients require insurance of course, but in the original mnemonic this was a get-out word to remind the trainee lender to consider what "security" of some appropriate description is needed.

Purple Shoots does not take formal security. We don't take Personal Guarantees. We don't secure assets in any way (although technically we do have a lien on any equipment bought). The "security" of our loans is in the small size of the loan: it is hardly enough with which to abscond.

There is also the question of trust. We interview all our applicants and can tell a lot from that meeting. Once we've gone through all the information given to us and have ultimately established trust in what we've seen and heard, we take into account the manner and attitude of the applicant. Trust goes the other way as well. We often get emails from successful applicants thanking us for the loan and saying that we are the only people to have shown trust in them for many years. That is a sad thing in many ways but it does set up a feeling of loyalty towards us that means we are more likely to be repaid.

We look for businesses that could work and people who can make them happen, regardless of where they're starting from or what has gone before.

STARTING SOMETHING WITH NOTHING

BOB SHEPHERD & KAREN DAVIES

Chapter Four
The Senses of Business

Throughout the day we use our five senses. Sight, smell, hearing, taste and touch are the five senses that we subconsciously use in proportion to our surroundings and our activities without thinking. Operating a business is a bit like that with various functions operating in every business in accordance with its circumstances, its size, its location and its people.

Here is a way of looking at any business: The size, sophistication and the numbers involved may alter, but these attributes should be there. They benefit the business; they don't work against it.

This is, in effect, the components of a successful business plan. The following chapters will show you how to become alive in your business, engaging with the outside world, taking note of what is going on and adapting what you do to act for the best.

We'll show you how important the internal feelings of the business are as well as its overall health. To achieve health and well-being in your business there are things to look out for, things to look after and things to avoid.

We all know when we're not feeling at our best. We all know when we need cheering up, when we need to slow down and when we need something to pick us up again. No one lives their life at a constant level with everything equally balanced. It's the same with a business. The business needs to be looked after, to be given the right sustenance and needs someone to ensure it's functioning well.

The business needs attention continually. It is a failing business that neglects any one aspect — often with over-attention to another. That leads to imbalance where parts of it become out of proportion in relation to the whole. Therefore, it's a complex thing to grow a business and keep that sense of proportion throughout. The business owner has many plates to spin!

This book can't tell you which spinning plates need attention — that's a matter for your own judgement. Each business is different even when they're ostensibly similar. No two plumbers are the same; no two corner shops are the same. It often comes down to the people involved, but there are also other forces at work (not least to do with location, the amount of investment, the timing and possibly the history of that business).

You can only deal with what you have. "We are where we are" is a phrase often trotted out in the business world when things are not ideal. Doing the best you can with what you have available must never be an excuse for not doing everything as well as you can. You may be able to change what you have available.

Your business reputation is key to your success and that is drawn from many things, which might include turning up on time, sweeping up after your work, reporting back on what you've done and a host of other things.

STARTING SOMETHING WITH NOTHING

BOB SHEPHERD & KAREN DAVIES

Chapter Five
Watching the People

Any business has people in it — some less obvious than others. Hopefully there will be customers and staff. There are people needed to service the business, the bank, the accountant, suppliers, delivery people and anyone involved. There is probably a landlord, the neighbouring businesses and other incidental folk. The point is that it is necessary to get on with all these people. They could and may well talk about you, or direct people to you. But along with all these people, there are other influences that matter or have mattered. Your character and demeanour have been steered by the contacts and people you have had up until now — family, friends, school and previous jobs. Whether they are good influences or not, their mark has been left upon you.

A lot of comedy has been based upon the unfortunate reactions displayed by people in everyday circumstances. You can't always get it right, but if you can get on with people, your business can also get on.

We sometimes get an approach where technically the business idea should work but the personality of the applicant doesn't fit. We do not "judge" anyone for being who they are. The point is, however, that they need to fit.

A man in jeans and T-shirt showing off two arms full of tattoos might be perfect for a tattoo artist, but not so great if he wants to run a café in a posh area or appeal to wealthy older people as a personal trainer.

> Make good relationships with anyone connected with your business. Present yourself in a way that will appeal to your customers.

LJ ran a very successful sweet shop for a number of years and then partnered with the shop next door so that between them they could expand their range and support each other. The partnership was informal and the partner turned out to be unreliable, letting her down and, in the end, forcing her out of her successful little shop.

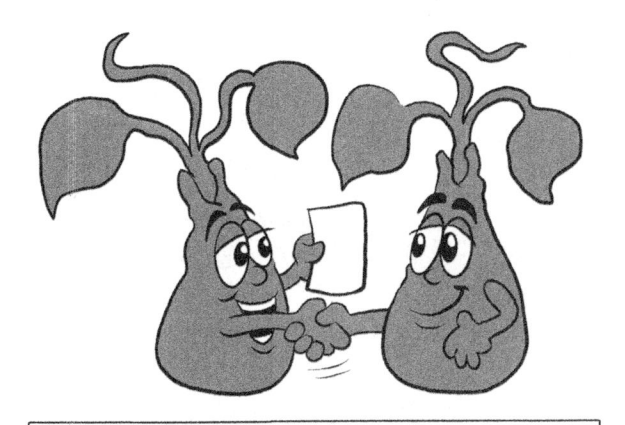

> Partnerships should have formal agreements – informal arrangements, even with friends, often go sour.

M and J wanted to take on a premises together: one would do hairdressing and the other would do beauty treatments. They were going to share the rent and other costs — they were good friends. However, very early on they fell out with each other, couldn't agree on how to run it or what costs were whose. Both businesses failed.

W set up a restaurant in partnership with the landlord of the premises who owned the building and ran a guesthouse above the restaurant. This was an informal relationship and the restaurant became untenable when the landlord refused to undertake expensive repairs unless W paid for them (which he couldn't). It ended the relationship and the business.

In many small businesses the business IS you. It not only

revolves around you and carries all your values and expectations, but it is also represented by you and how you deal with people on and off duty.

SUMMARY

- Think about all the people connected to your business;
- Present yourself and your business in a way that appeals to them;
- Work on good relationships with everyone;
- Have formal agreements, not friendly arrangements;

- Think about all the people connected to your business;

- Present yourself and your business in a way that appeals to them;

- Work on good relationships with everyone;

- Have formal agreements, not friendly arrangements.

Working with Friends and Family

At first glance this is an obvious and desirable path to take. There are indeed many successful family businesses or partnerships of one kind or another between friends.

You must enter these with your eyes open! Working together will change your relationship. It may even make it a better one.

As lenders and business consultants over the years, we've seen many family businesses. Sometimes the company has looked like this:

> Dad is the Managing Director. He is the ultimate decision-maker but is limited by his business upbringing and pulled by influences from younger family members.
>
> Grandad is the founder and still turns up three times a week because he draws a "consultancy fee" monthly. He sits in the corner for an hour or two and whilst maintaining that he doesn't want to interfere, does so by disapproving of much that is going on. Consequently, while paying dutiful attention, the rest of the family collectively conspire not to bother him with too much detail.
>
> The daughter is the company accountant but is not equipped to respond to the company's demands quickly or with an outside view. She gets called upon to help in all sorts of other areas, which she does.

The daughter and son are the ones who go out and get new clients. They are responsible for new initiatives but often can't take the rest of the family with them. Therefore, the initiatives don't always work as they could.

The son-in-law has been brought in at a senior level but, in reality, is the lowest in the pecking order. He is pushing for more online involvement.

It's a dysfunctional picture and looks stereotypical, but it was in fact a real situation. The frustrations and lack of cohesion boiled over regularly, adding a complication to the mix. The non-family staff worked around them, washing their hands of it all when they went home for tea. The family members were un-sackable but also not entirely suited to their roles.

In another case, Dad had built a good business and the son just saw it as hopelessly old-fashioned and out of date. Dad was resisting "new-fangled computerisation" to the despair of the son. Feeling embattled, he resisted any new attempts to market the business differently.

Family Funding

If you need money to set up, beware of family funding. Auntie's money or Gran's money is free ("pay me back when you can...") and the repayments are flexible. Unless properly agreed and set out formally however, misunderstandings and family resentments can easily develop. Such arrangements should always be on the basis that money provided might be lost all together and that every other family member knows about it. Obviously, you can still do your best to pay it back quickly but that's a goodwill thing.

If anything happens within the family while you have a loan outstanding, prepare for sparks to fly. You can't just pay it back, or you would have done so. Other people need help or can't understand why Gran can't afford to replace her washing machine or, worst of all, want their inheritance and won't feel patient or forbearing towards you.

Friends in Business

You are friends now and of a single mind. While that happy circumstance still exists, it's best to write down the arrangements. A Partnership Agreement or a Shareholders' Agreement for a limited company is always a sound idea. You should have everything set out in writing. If done properly, there can be no dispute because it is all there in front of you.

The agreement covers anything that might happen. This could be one person leaving or retiring. What is to be done about money invested in the company and can it be drawn out? Should the friendly relationship break down for any reason, an amicable or at least a civil break-up of the company can take place.

The same concerns apply, however, when you're dealing with friends in business — as customers, landlords, contractors, providers of work or any other capacity.

While it is true you want to deal with people you like (and so do they) it always has to be professional. To under-promise and over-deliver is something worth bearing in mind.

How to Check Out Customers or Business Partners

We all automatically "check out" everyone we meet. We make a quick assessment on first impressions, covering all manner of things. We are looking for safety in our dealings as well as social values. So, listen to yourself when you decide on your perceptions of someone.

You should do some other checks. Check online that they are as they say they are and that they fit your focus of interest. What you find may satisfy you. Don't forget that you can probably discount the best and worst reviews you find.

Reference to others who have used them may count for you. An introduction is great, but your introducer is not the trading partner you seek and there is only so much you can ask. Equally, you can hardly go back to your introducer and blame him if their experience turns out to be better than yours.

The days when you could get a bank reference have gone, although technically it is still possible. It was only ever an indication however, but reassuring, nevertheless.

B wanted to engage with a small building firm for some groundworks and construction of some outbuildings. A friend posted pictures on Facebook of some work he had had done and he was asked for details. Given the name and phone number and a specific recommendation, B went looking online. There was nothing commercial and no presence at all, but there was an indication that the builder was the grandson of his friend's wife. A phone call and a meeting explained some of the gaps. The attitude and knowledge of the builder fitted and a quote was agreed.

Not everyone is online (although arguably they should be). In this case, the builder has so much work by personal recommendation that he didn't have the time or see the necessity to spend time building a profile online.

If you are regularly engaging with other companies, you may like to register as a user of one of the credit agencies which will give you information from the public records.

Simple procedures will protect you as well. Notice, for example, that when you take your car to the garage for work to be done, you pay your bill at the desk before they give you your keys back.

Check what similar businesses to your own do and consider the security they employ. Pre-payments, part or stage payments may be appropriate.

BOB SHEPHERD & KAREN DAVIES

Chapter Six
Shouting to the Outside World

If you tell no one you are there, you can't expect any interest. Setting up a business is rarely a case of opening the door on a Monday morning and watching your customers stream through the door.

There are a lot of things to consider and the more efficiently you address them, the better. Things like Marketing, PR, Branding, Networking, Advertising and Market Placement are all part of "Shouting to the Outside World!"

Whatever you do needs to be tempered by the budget, the audience, the location and a need to be attractive, welcoming and engaging. We've seen businesses who say they have a wonderful marketing plan, but that they can't afford it at the moment. That is no plan at all then! Everything needs to be in proportion to the available resources. But there must ALWAYS be marketing.

Marketing

Keep it in proportion! Consider the sort of customers you're trying to attract. Consider what others do with similar businesses. You don't necessarily want to do the same, but you can learn lessons from what they did. What you do is a mixture of what is likely to be effective and what you can afford within the scope of your business resources. That expensive TV campaign may not be necessary or even a good idea!

For example, a business producing honey products appeared on a popular television programme which excited many orders. It gave wonderful exposure but caused a panic at the processing plant when they realised that they had insufficient labels and jars and not enough people to produce their finished goods for the orders that were flooding in. The problems arose all along the production process.

We've seen shops fail, citing too few customers to make it viable. In truth, because of costs and available finance, they had opted for a poor location with not enough passing customers. In that situation, they needed to do more marketing to bring people to them or add deliveries or online sales.

Keeping it simple may suggest that cards on the noticeboards of local shops, pubs and clubs may be the right thing for you. Some corner newsagents still run a board with notices on it for a small fee. In some communities, that may work very well. A local magazine may be available or a local website or Facebook page or group. If you consider that a leaflet distribution may be a good thing to do, then some things may be appropriate to consider. This applies to other forms of communication also.

The collateral, as it is called, which is the material you are distributing, needs to be carefully put together. Don't use too many words and add big clear contact numbers with a quick summary of the kind of service you offer (not too much detail). Attractive illustrations are useful. Font size and types should be clear and limited. If it looks too busy, it will not be read.

Thereafter, choose a delivery firm that knows your area and checks its deliveries are made (unless you're doing it yourself). Make sure also that they limit their deliveries. Observation of your own letterbox will show you that the A4 pizza place leaflet actually has all the other leaflets inside it. They mostly go straight into the bin — yours could too (even if individually pushed through your letterbox)!

> Deliver leaflets more than once!

Therefore, send out another in three weeks and repeat it after three more weeks. By the time it has passed quickly before their eyes, your potential customer will be thinking: "I have heard of them somewhere" and may take a look or keep the leaflet on the kitchen noticeboard.

If you don't have it professionally designed, have your leaflet or material seen by someone else. The unintentional typo or the wrong phone number or something silly can easily be read over by you if you've written it.

The principle applies to all communication. Whatever you think you've said, the material is received by someone else. They have all their interests, experiences and prejudices drawn from many sources to influence the way they interpret and understand what you've said. You have no idea what they may be. Clear communication is a complicated thing. So take another look at your emails, your posters, your voicemail, your Facebook posts, LinkedIn posts, your website, etc.

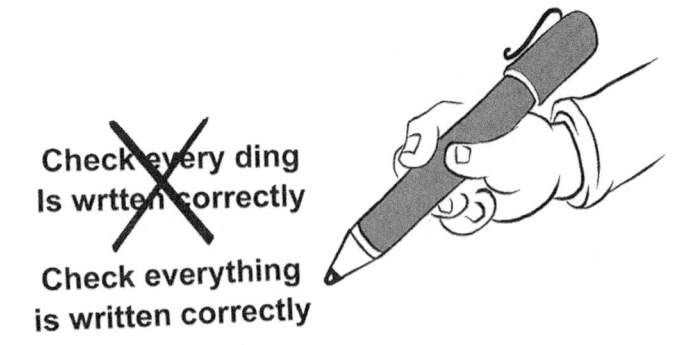

~~Check every ding
Is wrtten correctly~~

**Check everything
is written correctly**

Other Communication – Presentation

Anything written is potentially a communication to the outside world. Care must be taken in all of it as we have seen. However, are other forms need care too. Your business needs to give a positive impression that attracts potential customers. The way things look matters, as well as the way it's positioned.

We helped a local shop that was at one end of a long street in a South Wales Valleys' town. Their main competition was at the other end of that street some quarter of a mile away. Both sold similar things, both had a liquor licence and both sold magazines and newspapers. Both were open at similar hours and it seemed that whichever was nearest would probably get the trade.

How was our client going to develop? The answer was to create a better environment for sales. The newspapers near the door and the till had a handy shelf running along below so multi-pack cans of beer could go there. When people turned up for their paper they were presented with beers and lagers as they reached for a paper. It was the same principle as having sweets by the till in a supermarket. The goods in the rest of the shop were rearranged into a more logical sequence. A simple piece of reorganisation increased turnover.

Other forms of communication also have to do with presentation. If something looks the part, it is so much better (this applies whether or not you are selling goods or services). The van that turns up at your door doesn't have to look like an MOT failure. The operator or shop assistant (or you) should dress appropriately for the service or environment.

In an old-fashioned town, newsagents still performed as they had for years. People still came in to pay their newspaper bills. More remarkably perhaps, people still came in to buy sixty or eighty cigarettes a day. The shop was set out so that the customer had to walk the length of the shop to get to the counter at the far end. That means they would pass all kinds of opportunistic "reminder" purchases on the way: chocolates, greetings cards, stationery as well as magazines. The owners walked in the front every day and spent their day on and around the counter, failing to notice that the view from the pavement outside had become dire. The shop looked as if it was soon going to close but from the counter end it looked fine. Always look from your customers' point of view!

A new business was being set up to be a specialist recruitment service. Technically, the owner's voicemail contained all the necessary information. However, the owner had written it out to make sure it was right and had then recorded it. When she said, "Leave me your number and I shall get back to you," it was delivered as a statement and not an invitation. If she had only changed the tone to an inviting constructional call to action, it would've been so much better. On the other hand, it's very important to have a voicemail on your phone, thanking the caller for ringing and inviting them to leave their name and number. It is equally important to check your phone for messages and return them as soon as possible — customers respond well if they think you want them to.

> Think about the impression
> you are giving your customers

Can you present your business in a better way? Are your emails properly written and do they have contact details that are well presented? Do you and/or your staff respond in a helpful and timely manner?

An interesting exercise is to consider why you use certain shops, garages or other places. The presentation is a matter of balance over a number of factors. The importance may alter according to the service and in one case the location for example, may perhaps trump the lack of variety. The opening hours may make your trip worthwhile, meaning you're happy to compromise on some other aspect. Any one aspect may be enough to put you off.

- Location
- Opening hours
- Availability
- Ease of access
- Parking
- Variety and display
- Staff attitude
- Cleanliness
- Price level
- Slow/quick service

An interesting example occurred at a financial services counter: "Do you have foreign currency on your till?" was the question. "No, but they do have at the Post Office," was the helpful answer.

Where is that customer going to go for their currency next time? Very likely to the Post Office. It would've been better to have answered, "If you let me know what you need, we can have it delivered here or to your home by tomorrow." It's rare for currency to be required immediately. Ignoring the question's content would not seem rude or unhelpful — rather the opposite!

Always answer any question in the affirmative. The answer is never what you can't do, but rather what you can. This takes practice, but it's an important principle. We

STARTING SOMETHING WITH NOTHING

are never absolutely unable to help; we can f
what we can do. "If you leave it with us, we can g
priority on Wednesday as soon as the parts have arr
and phone you when it's ready for collection." Th
sounds as if you're doing your best to sort something out.
It doesn't sound like you're saying, "You picked a bad day
to bring this in, mate. We can't do anything until
Wednesday and then you'll be lucky."

A backstreet garage was a typical "grease monkey" environment. The boss, realising that at least half the potential cars on the road were driven by women, decided to have a tidy-up and a rebrand. They changed the name to something that sounded friendly and atmospheric. They created a clean waiting-and-service area. Unfortunately, the phone was answered a hundred

...eone who was in the middle of ...nd who put down his tools on the ...e keys of the computer and the ...mechanics brought in their fish-...ers in the bin. The result was a ...ormer state very quickly. The ... jumbled together and lost its appeal. The place smelled of grease, damp and fish-and-chips. The leopards had reverted to their spots.

Branding

Branding is simply everything that you present to the outside world. It is so much more than the logo and the headed paper banner. It includes the whole backdrop to your business as viewed from outside.

Everything from your voicemail and email signature to the way you present your business and the adverts and videos you make to publicise things: all have your branding at heart!

It needs to be consistent, express your values and your whole way of doing things. None of it sells anything for you directly. It's more a case that not getting it right will impede any sales effort. So look to every way your business interacts with the outside world. Ensure the picture presented is consistent.

Check everything written: invoices, emails, business cards, letters, notes and tickets of any sort; social media posts, websites, business name, URL, online index references, etc.

Check everything visual: vehicles, clothing/uniform, wrapping, the website, the Facebook page, Twitter, LinkedIn, etc.

Check everything verbal: voicemail, how the phone is answered, introductory patter, networking elevator pitch, videos, etc.

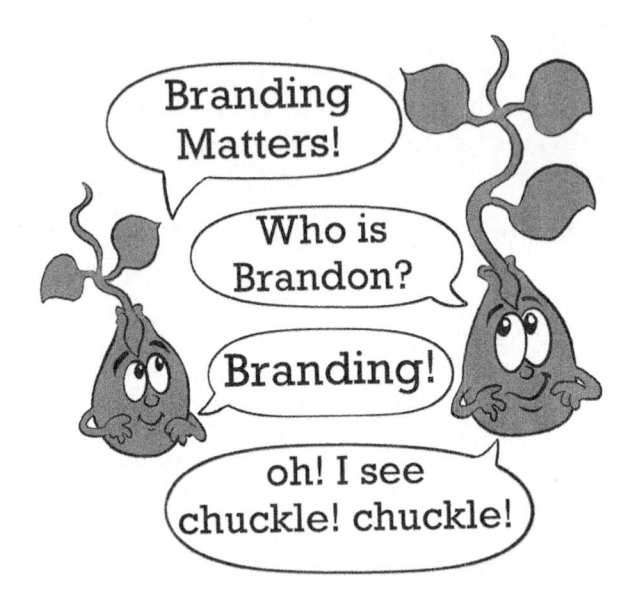

> Branding Matters!
>
> Who is Brandon?
>
> Branding!
>
> oh! I see chuckle! chuckle!

Branding matters and is more than just your logo

Networking

As part of the backdrop and the search for customers, most businesses could benefit from networking. People new to business are often nervous of networking but the truth is many people in networking groups find it just as difficult and everyone wants newcomers to feel welcome.

When you network, it isn't with the purpose to sell anything. It's to raise a profile and become known, liked and trusted. Good business follows. In normal times there are breakfast meetings and others for small businesses that follow a pattern. There's a period of general chat while everyone who has booked arrives. Then, there's a formal introduction by the host who is running the meeting. Sometimes a meal is involved followed by a round of personal short presentations from those present. This is called your "elevator pitch" (more about that in a moment). Usually there's a short talk from a member or special guest and then a chance to talk further to anyone you have identified who might be particularly interested.

Your agenda should not be to "work the room" in a cynical round of quick introductions. Rather, your intention should be to strike up a relationship with two or three present and follow that up afterwards. From casual conversations, things develop. It follows that a general question to anyone such as "How is it going?" may be sufficient to get a conversation going and there may be something there that you can help with.

At a good meeting, you will hear conversations about anything but business going on, plenty of laughter and friendships forming.

> Networking gets you friends, collaborators and supporters and helps make your business known. Lots of people struggle with it – you aren't alone if you're nervous.

Your "elevator pitch" is an interesting concept and once you've grasped it then you can adapt it and use it formally or casually; at length or in short bursts. The term comes from a concept that you should be able to sum up your business in a short conversation lasting the time it takes to be in a lift (elevator). To do this is more complicated than it sounds.

In a few short sentences you will have your whole business on display, incorporating your values, your service, the benefits of what you do and a door open for further interest to come in.

It's a lot to encompass within a few short phrases, but once you've done it, you've also sorted out your business approach.

Follow this framework:

> You know when...
>
> What I do...
>
> The result is...
>
> The benefits are...

You don't need to use those words but express that thought.

"You know when" sets the scene for your business and describes the setting in which you work in that arena.

"What I do" shows how you tackle the issues you have described above.

"The result is": A short outcome from the intervention you make.

"The benefits are": This is where the attractiveness of what you do is displayed.

People only buy if there's a perceived benefit for them in doing so. Sometimes that is very simple. At the other end of the scale the perceived benefits are complex and individual.

Your elevator pitch can be used casually in response to a conversational question or it can be expanded into a talk about your business. Once the basis of it is there, you can easily adapt it. We suggest that you get a sheet of paper and write out the answers to the four points described above. Then get another sheet and do it again. Then put those aside and stand before a mirror and present it to yourself. Another version will emerge. If you need to limit it to about one minute, make sure you time your delivery. Once you've presented it a couple of times, a standard version will emerge. It needs to be easy to say and flow naturally. When it becomes automatic, you will find you can adapt it to answer a more specific question and to fit some different circumstance or to present over different periods of time as required. It will come over naturally and in a relaxed way — which is what you want.

> **Work out your elevator pitch and practice it.**

The outcomes per meeting can't be measured. You sometimes hear people say that they have been to three meetings and got nothing from it. That just says they have approached it wrongly or, in some way, failed to use the opportunity properly.

Speak up, speak with confidence and become known as the "person who does" in your particular context. The openings will then emerge. Be selective about giving out your cards. Try giving a card to someone you've had a good conversation with. That way your card becomes a "calling card" of some value, rather than one of a pocketful of cards for whom they can't remember the face that goes with it.

Have a pop-up banner to stand in front of when you talk. Have some leaflets to put out on a table if that is encouraged. Spread your influence gently, with value and good humour. Nobody likes to feel they have been used by someone only interested in selling them something. Follow up the good conversations you have had. Be more interested in them and you will spot the good opportunities.

If you can get to do a talk then so much the better. The owner of a will-writing business hawked a talk with slides around a circuit of local clubs and societies including WI ("Women's Institute"), book clubs and other local societies. After his talk the audience felt they knew him well, trusted him and laughed at some of his stories. He reckoned about twenty per cent booked him to come and see them afterwards and from there, they referred their families to his services.

Some networking meetings are not so useful. Just because it is called "the so-and-so business club" doesn't mean it is good for you. Some are simply an opportunity to take a table of guests, see a well-known face, give a talk and come away with no real networking done. If you make enquiries first, you should be able to pick these out. Your best opportunities come by being there for the chat before the meeting gets going and being there for the wind-down afterwards. A meeting where everyone heads for the door when it is finished has not been a good meeting.

Online networking has been more in evidence since the Covid lockdowns. That shows how important networking is to a business. The principles are similar but there are differences. It is harder to remember people met this way, because the social clues are not there to be seen so well. The opportunities to bump into people are not so good and you can't control who you talk to so well. On the other hand, people can be there from far and wide who wouldn't normally make the long journey. That may or may not be useful to you and depends on your business and its comfortable and sensible reach.

Costs are another variable. Online meetings are much cheaper. Watch the cost but make no mistake: Networking is a powerful force. The referrals may come in years later — in some cases once you are known.

PR

Public Relations is really anything that gets you out in the media. An article in a newspaper or magazine about your business can be very effective — interviews on radio or appearances on TV even more so. National publicity is difficult to achieve. Sadly, the press aren't excited by good news stories and rarely publish them (local press being an exception to this rule). So if you have a good client story or something to say as a local business to your local community, local papers are good. The best way to have items published is to use a PR person. There are some good small businesses that do this — no need to engage Saatchi and Saatchi. However, whoever you use, there is a cost.

PR can also be achieved through events (attending exhibitions or even running your own event).

Social Media and Websites

Social media is a free form of marketing which can be used to great benefit. There are a number of platforms: The big four at the moment are Twitter (now renamed "X"), LinkedIn, Facebook and Instagram. With all of them, the key is to be consistent in how you write your messages but also with how consistently you do it. The odd post every now and then won't cut it: It needs to be frequent and regular to be really effective.

The platform you use will depend on your business and who your customers are. As a general rule, Instagram tends to be for more visual businesses and is used by a younger demographic. Facebook has a wider age range and tends to be more informal. LinkedIn is much more business-oriented (it works in a similar way to Facebook) with regular posts and commenting on other's posts while building connections. Twitter (or "X"), although dominated a bit by celebrities and public sector/government people, can be a very useful tool in becoming more widely known and for sharing information about your business (although this has declined recently with Threads emerging as a potential alternative).

If you have accounts with any or all of the above, you need them to work together and to point people towards your website or Facebook page. Include links to it whenever you can.

When you're posting, try to post a mix of personal anecdotes, information about your business and opinions or comments about the industry you are working in. Remember that potential customers or funders will check out your online presence — be careful what you post.

Your business may not need a website to start with, but you must have some sort of online presence because everyone looks for that these days. If there is no website, have a Facebook page which gives information about your business and include, if you can, pictures of your work and testimonials from happy customers.

Important Points

Marketing: Keep doing it, even when you're busy.

Branding: It matters and it's more than just a logo.

Leaflets: Check them carefully for typos and deliver them more than once.

Networking: It's scary, but important.

PR: Start with the local press.

Social media: It's free marketing — use it to the full.

Website/Facebook page: You must have an online presence.

"Shh-I'm doing a video for Instagram

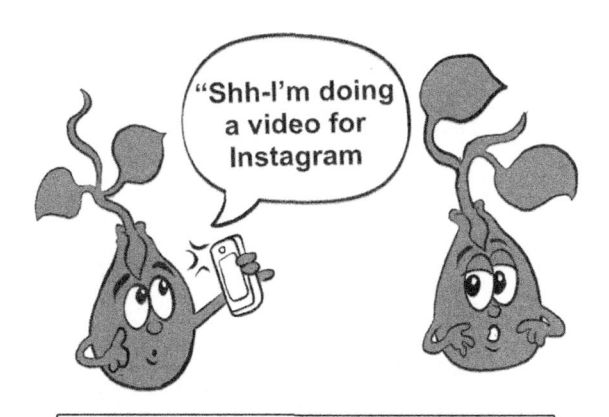

Actively posting on social media and pointing people to your website and Facebook page is free and effective – and more effective the more you do it.

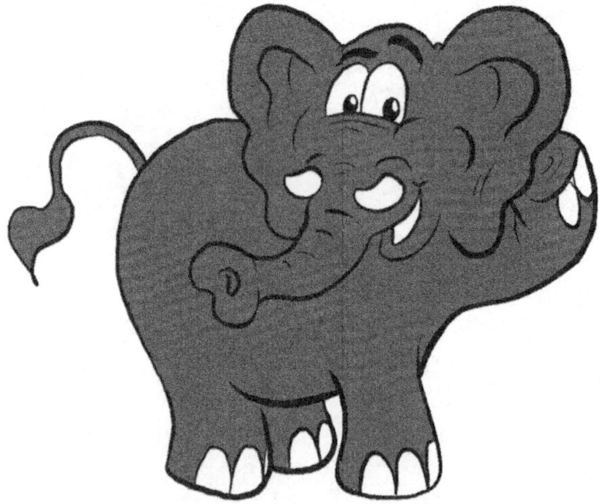

Chapter Seven
Listening to the Outside World

What your competitors do is important. You don't have to do the same as they, but they may have trodden your path before. Therefore, take note and learn from them — free of charge!

Once set up, you will find it hard to gain an outside view of your business. Getting feedback or testimonials is one way. Engaging on social media is another. A survey may be useful but ultimately sales is your measure.

Handling Complaints

Nobody wants complaints so try to avoid giving cause! However, receiving a complaint is a chance to engage with a customer and if you can turn a complaint into a customer who thinks you're great and will come back to you, then you've done a good job.

There are some important markers to put down when you have a complaint. Remember your values and reputation are at stake and this is your chance to put it right.

Some suggestions:

- Acknowledge the complaint. Respond immediately in some way or at least on the same day, even if it's to hold the position while you investigate further.

- Assume the complaint is valid. Nothing is guaranteed to wind up the complainant more than open disbelief.

- Never accuse the complainant of causing the issue (at least not initially).

- Check the substance of the complaint.

- Even if it isn't correct, find a way of dealing with the problem as it has emerged.

- Consider some concession that makes up for the unmet expectation.

- If justified, consider a free reward of some kind as a goodwill gesture.

The problem is that complaints stay in existence for future anecdotes for many years, even if put right.

"I got 450 quid out of [a certain Insurance company] when I complained." This sounds great and adds importance to the personality recounting the tale in years to come. In fact the £450 was an overcharge and not a goodwill payment. All that happened really was that the error was adjusted to what it should have been. Another part of this particular true story is that after unsuccessfully attempting to attract attention to his complaint from a bureaucratic system, the complainer put a note on "X." The response was immediate and cut through a lot of red tape to deal quickly with the matter. Do the insurance company get credit for that? Not really: "It was only when I put something on 'X' that I got any sense out of anyone."

Another tale shows how badly a complaint can be handled:

A friend L was in the country on business for two months — just long enough to make it worthwhile getting a local mobile phone. B took L into a well-known "High Street" phone retailer and a suitable mobile phone was purchased "Pay-as-you-Go." Having taken it away to a nearby café, it became clear that the phone was defective. They went back to the shop and were met by a young assistant.

"You must have done something to it..." This wasn't the best response. "These never go wrong. I can't refund you just like that..." So it went on. In front of a shop full of waiting customers the worst customer service was on show with a row developing. Clearly, there was a visible need for staff training. By the time a senior got involved there was damage to be undone and feathers to be unruffled. As a manager you never want to be seen knocking your staff over, so a way had to be found to offer sufficient repair to the customer's device and to retain the dignity of the shop. The story lives on some years later.

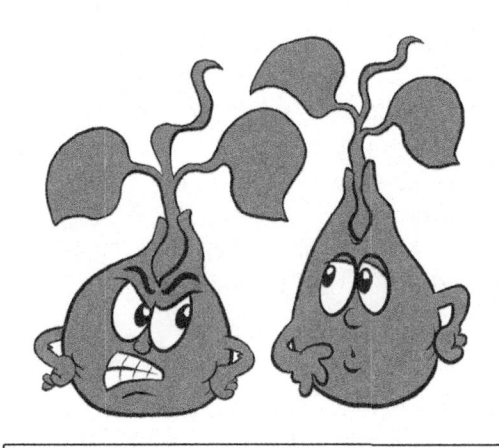

> Respond to complaints immediately – and act as if the customer is right until you find otherwise.

Keeping Up to Date with Your Market

Feedback and suggestions should always be welcome. It's important for your work to keep up with the Trade press and online groups. It is important to pick up on new innovations in equipment. Window cleaners no longer use buckets and a ladder. Many now have a tank of distilled water in a van and a long brush that feeds water and cleaning fluid to the upstairs storey windows.

Rather than keeping up with your market, you might think that it's better to get ahead of your market if you can. That is a brave and spirited thing to do, but not always easy. Very often the only difference between some businesses and yours is the quality of delivery of service. It isn't hard to achieve this, but it can be hard to maintain it. Think about the times when you've received exceptional service. How does that make you feel? Will you go back to them?

Smaller businesses can often pride themselves on their service while larger businesses struggle. That is simply a function of the number of people involved in the chain of delivery. Look after your people and it will pay off. All the marketing and training expense in the world will go out of the window on a bad day if the person handling a new enquiry (on a desk, by phone or any other method) is in a bad mood and giving out poor impressions.

It's an old lesson. The person at the reception desk or answering the phone should not be the newest junior. Their role is crucial to the future business of the company.

Professional offices used to adopt that approach in banks, as solicitors or accountants. The thinking was that the technical expertise was required on the senior floor and not on reception (who only had to field a call and pass it on).

DKC was a small manufacturing company having a cash-flow crisis. They had a good product and had open days, exhibitions and some sales and the owner was justifiably proud of what he had achieved. However, he wasn't the man who should have been doing the selling. He had a large list of potential buyers who had expressed interest but with whom he had never followed up because he didn't have time. Had he sold products consistently, he would not be having a cash-flow crisis. It was a management and marketing issue — not a financial one — and easily resolved by the personable lady on reception who had time and charm to talk to the customers and establish a rapport. Once she had been given some training, the problem resolved itself because she did the selling and the "boss" could get on with organising the workflow.

Feedback

Feedback is a wonderful thing and should be sought after at every opportunity. Online listings or presence should be supported with a lot of feedback — the more the better. Websites should have feedback shown where possible and every chance to publish good feedback should be taken. More extensive feedback can be quoted in publicity booklets and other material. Do keep an eye on what is posted, however, in case of rogue feedback appearing. It is common for competitors to post negative feedback or false testimonials. There's always that eccentric customer who has a grudge against the world. The problem is that most feedback stays in place for others to see in future.

There are one or two feedback-handling companies that seek testimonials for you and vet incoming ratings.

Business Jargon

Corporate Sales Speak and Management Speak and their cousins are alive and well.

There's a case for jargon and short-hand speech within an industry and its peers. When that spills out to a wider audience, it can be frustrating or amusing (depending on your viewpoint). We are not saying that language should always be plain (although that can be admirable on occasion). There are many cases for using the rich heritage of the English language to create effect or to give slant or emphasis to make a point.

However, those who trot out business clichés raise questions about their own understanding of the subject and their own security within their business world. Are they trying to impress? Are they sheltering behind familiar club or tribal terms to show they belong? It must begin somewhere and it's amusing to see people in an audience making a discreet note with an obvious intention of using those phrases themselves later (or maybe of finding out what they actually mean).

Some of the best/worst examples we've recently come across are:

- "Within the SME landscape..."
- "Build new solutions in the alternative space..."
- "Create an atmosphere for solutionising the problems..."
- "...that is less, on a relative basis."
- "What are the key take-aways?"
- "Let's see what that scenario looks like..."

You get the idea. Some of them are quite clearly nonsense. Some other examples were quite clever at first but have now been done to death!

We all use idiomatic or useful little phrases as part of our speech, but some of these should never achieve currency and do say more about the user than they should be pleased about.

You do, however, want to understand what the business world is talking about. Useful phrases for the business user are the more technical ones:

Business Plan and Cash Flow Forecast are referred to elsewhere. Break-even is simply the point at which your business is going well enough to make you some spare money. There are ways of calculating this. Understand the term "turnover" and most importantly that it isn't the same as profit. Depreciation is an accounting term which allows you to write-off some profit in order to set it aside for the replacement of a large item.

B2B/B2C, margins/profit margin, equity, return on investment, profit and loss, liabilities and the difference between revenue money and capital money are all worth understanding. Don't get too hung up on these things. You can always look them up. It is useful to develop a nose for pretentious business speak. Generally, we can do without it. Sometimes it's funny, but don't let it get in the way of good business.

SUMMARY

- Keep up to date with your industry and with things going on in the world that might affect it.

- Ask for feedback — testimonials etc. — and publicise it.

- Handle complaints sensitively.

- Don't let business jargon, and people who use it, put you off.

STARTING SOMETHING WITH NOTHING

BOB SHEPHERD & KAREN DAVIES

Chapter Eight
Watching the Money

Money is the oil that keeps the engine running. It used to be a popular thing to say, "Cash is King." That isn't quite true, because if you neglect the rest of the business and pay too much attention to the cash, then it won't work. Your business needs to be in proportion.

There are many aspects to money and it's worth considering some of them for a moment. In general terms there are two types of money — Capital and Revenue.

Capital: This is your set-up money, money for equipment, money to establish the business or enlarge some activity. It's a once-off spend each time and you won't see money back directly, unless you sell the piece of equipment or perhaps the business.

Revenue: This is your day-to-day spendings that works round the system and comes back in to keep things running (staff costs, electricity, gas, rent, insurance etc). It circulates.

The Cash Cycle

It's important that money circulates sufficiently well for a business to keep running. Whether the business is a service or a manufacturing process, the principle is the same. Once the tools, equipment and base of the business is established, then money is spent to:

- create interest and attract orders for work;
- do the work;
- deliver things in some way;
- wait for payment to be received and processed;
- pay the workforce;
- pay for overheads to enable more work to be done in future.

This is happening on a continual basis, of course. It isn't a one-by-one job and not always in a steady stream (especially at the beginning). One mistake that is made by those who are contractors is to go after and be delighted in the big jobs rather than a lot of little jobs. Big jobs mean that your van is parked in one place for a long time and not working for you and you are not seen out and about. It may mean that you have to keep going for some while until payment is made. It means the risk is concentrated. So if there's any argument about the work or disagreement about payment in some way, then a large amount is at stake.

It's much better to have a number of smaller jobs each with the same risks but a smaller part of what you do. This could result in more people who speak well of you and more locations for your sign-written van to be seen and to be busy. There could be more chances perhaps for neighbours — or other people — to see you and just ask for some help...

A small two-man landscaping and gardening business was delighted to report they had landed a ten-week prestigious contract to substantially remodel the gardens and grounds of a large house belonging to a doctor. Weekly stage payments were to be made. The profit from the job would therefore all be in the final couple of payments. Having supplied all the materials and hired equipment, the work progressed well until the eighth week when the doctor expressed dissatisfaction with the job and an argument developed. The partnership would/could not continue working unless they were paid. The doctor would not pay for work when he wasn't happy. There are remedies available to the firm who had a contract after all, but any enforcement would be lengthy and expensive. As a result, they had worked hard for minimum pay, had been off the road and not seen for effectively eight weeks, had been lucky to come out of it even with costs and had a potential damaged reputation brewing. Even if the doctor didn't actively talk poorly of them, they'd walked off a job without finishing it. It was certainly unfair and a disaster.

The "Admin"

All businesses have some administration tasks – "admin." This is any work essential to the business for which you are not directly paid. It might include travel, going to the bank, paying bills, issuing invoices, ordering supplies or hiring equipment. It could also be getting equipment repaired or serviced. It includes ordering new cartridges for the printer. These are big and small tasks that are essential for the well-being and continuance of the business. It includes bookkeeping and doing the tax returns and maybe the returns to Companies House (more on all this later). If the business is a little bigger, then there are staff to look after, holidays and sickness to organise cover for and all the management tasks needed to present a workforce in a good way. Any business spends around a third of its time in doing some form of admin.

That implies that the ability of the business to do paid work is reduced by a third. It gets more complicated than that because we have excluded speculative work from the term. You don't have to do that because speculative work is similarly not earning money directly. This includes seeing people about work, making enquiries and putting out communications explaining that you're available for what you do – "marketing," if you like.

In most small businesses another third of available time is spent in speculative activity. This happens along with admin accounts for up to two thirds of the time available or at least something between half and two thirds of the time. Time is your biggest resource. This isn't often realised.

Put another way, a one-man small business can only earn for around fourteen hours a week, sensibly. A two-man business where they work together is no better, because although the work is done more quickly with two, there is more inefficiency involved; more standing around waiting. That gain with two is not a compensation for all the hours lost where two are travelling or seeing people or waiting around.

> It's not just about being paid for the work you do – the money you earn has to cover the time you spend getting work and all the related admin tasks.

Pricing

What you charge for your work is crucial to get right. In many businesses, it's hard to increase it later. We see many businesses undercharging because they undervalue themselves and because they fear that too high a price will mean they don't get work. Fundamentally, your price must cover all your costs (including an income for yourself) or there is no point doing the work.

You can't take a wage for the work and divide it by around forty hours a week and say that is your price. Similarly, if you employ anyone the work they do should bring in at least three times in value of their salary/wage. A calculation has to be made. You need to consider also that the employee gets paid for thirty five to forty hours a week if full-time (whether there is enough work to fill that time or not). Many people do not understand why a contractor of any sort has a much higher pay rate than an employed person but this is why. Two examples may illustrate the problem.

A solicitor working in the provinces (not the London area where fees are double at least, but for exactly the same reasons of sheer cost) might typically charge £400-£600 per hour for his services or maybe £350 for writing a letter on your behalf. That income covers preparation time, admin time, speculative work time, other work for which (for various reasons) he/she has not been paid; employment of staff to clean, expenses in running the office, staff on reception, vehicles, premises costs, depreciation of assets, computers, phones, insurances and professional indemnities (which may be several tens of thousands of pound per year), professional costs, tax and some recompense for not being able to earn anything until completing education and exams that took them into their twenties. Now the fees don't look so far-fetched.

GL, a qualified engineer was employed in a firm set up recently to do house and property surveys – mainly for mortgage. A typical fee for the work was £450 which was the "going rate." As the business was new with limited resources, only three people besides the owner were involved with one employed solely on bringing in work. As such, they were more than usually pushed by demands that meant more work than they could reasonably manage.

Typically, a survey takes from two hours to four hours, with a report to do that taking as long again. With work coming in from all over South Wales, travel times could be anything from an hour to two and a half hours and then back again. Sometimes a detour was required to fetch keys to gain access and then return them again. In single numbers one person could do between four and seven surveys a week, depending on the locations. Fed up with the workload, GL approached us to consider "going at it alone." Five minutes' calculation showed him that it was not viable and that he needed six or seven employees to achieve a working load that would be reasonable and pay a viable income. He returned to work happier with an understanding of the problem. The only way it was working is with efficiencies gained from diary management, location scheduling and taking shortcuts in the reports by cutting and pasting standard paragraphs and using previous reports as a template. GL was head-hunted soon after by a firm that was better resourced.

How is Your Pricing Made Up?

Your pricing should cover your expenditure, your time, plus some profit. There's nothing wrong with making a profit. Indeed it's essential to make some profit to provide for future operations.

It's a complicated calculation. If you're producing a physical product, you'll have the cost of the materials, packaging and delivery, to which you must calculate some proportion of the equipment you have used plus promotion and premises costs and allowance for your time and whoever else may be involved.

If you're providing a service, then you have the costs of doing so which may include some equipment, travel, promotion costs and time involved. This isn't simple at all. How much is your time worth? As we've said before you may have established an hourly rate for your time. If you also have employees, then their costs must be included as well.

For simple one-man businesses, a fairly arbitrary approach may still be appropriate, working on what you want to have as take home pay from your business. It can't be a normal salary divided by a (say) forty-hour week. It may be helpful to reference back to the "third/third/third" principle discussed earlier.

CC was operating a garden services business across a wide district. At the time she was charging her clients £15 per hour, simply on the basis that a local jobbing gardener's price was that. Wondering why she was struggling to make ends meet, despite having a good number of customers we pointed out some obvious flaws in her pricing:

She was driving an old high-top Transit van and servicing an area of some forty miles by fifteen. This means there was often travel time between jobs and diary management was crucial. The van was old and keeping up with repairs and servicing, MOTs, tyres, exhausts, vehicle depreciation etc. was costly also. The simple cost of fuel alone was substantial.

She was making no allowance for seeking business or allowance for lost business or discounts given for any reason. Small amounts of materials weren't being charged for either: compost, sprays, netting, etc. where she had some available. Travel was not simply turning up at a job. It should make allowances for any trips out to get supplies or materials during the job.

In short, any money was going before she could pay herself. At this conclusion you can decide that either your pricing has to be more realistic or you should do something else.

Another example was LP's café. It was well-run and busy but she was losing money. We had a closer look at her pricing: it was low but she protested that she was operating in a poor area and no one would pay more. A look at what was included in some of her products provided the answer. For example, a breakfast bap (breadroll) for £3.99 contained so many ingredients that there was almost no margin on it. That meant that there was nothing to cover the cost of preparing it, paying staff to serve it etc. The solution was to reduce what was in it slightly but keep the price the same: one sausage (not three), two rashers of bacon (not three) etc. It was a small tweak, but enough to turn it around.

Make sure ALL your costs are covered in the price.
People almost never buy the cheapest.

Sometimes your market decides the price for you, but this is most unfortunate. In recent years there have been times when dairy farmers were producing milk at a loss, with the price being dictated by the large supermarkets. Such a position is unsustainable. The farm couldn't suddenly stop production or withhold supply or even choose who the customers should be in large part. Fortunately the supermarkets realised they were strangling the supplier and have moderated their approach. Always consider the usual cost of your product to the general public, but then decide if you wish to compete or wish to differentiate in some way.

The most successful businesses set their own prices and when a reputation is established, can be in a market that isn't "price sensitive." Why do we pay more for branded products? Put another way, why is the supermarket own brand of exactly the same product alongside so much cheaper? Very often you can tell by the packaging that it's precisely the same product. Supermarkets produce nothing. It's all done by the original manufacturers.

Another interesting question is why the supermarket will continue to sell the brand name alongside their own cheaper product. One answer is that it shows their own brand to advantage, but also that some customers continue to be happy to pay more for a brand they recognise and trust.

Overheads

When you calculate your price you must make allowances for overheads. These are the costs of you running that business. It's somewhat independent of the number of goods or client invoices you produce. In that those costs will be there, is some measure even if you do no business.

Things like rent and rates are obvious ones. Premises and staff costs are always the largest items in a business' accounts. If there are no premises and you're working from home, you still have some costs but you have some tax allowances you can claim as well. Overheads include incidental costs that happen anyway almost regardless of the number of invoices you issue. They do have some relationship in so far as the more work you do, the more background costs there will be.

The best course for the new business is to work out a sum per hour that needs to be charged for overheads. You can only do this once the workflow has achieved a more reliable volume, but you can look ahead and calculate what it will become. That means your price per hour (or per product for example), now becomes your allowance for overheads, plus your direct costs, plus your time and plus a profit. The profit is needed to enable you to grow the business or plan for replacing large items – even to reinvest in your community if you don't want to keep it yourself.

It may be a loading of thirty or forty per cent and many new businesses feel guilty charging for something they don't have evidence for directly. Remember though, it's a cushion against incidental costs and unforeseen future events.

Rounding Up or Down

Once you've arrived at a price you may feel it looks like a silly figure. Rounding up to the nearest ten pounds is a possible rule that you can follow. If you feel that the job you are pricing is an introduction to much more work, you might feel you can round down the price to appear more attractive. Be careful that you're not setting a precedent though. When the repeat order comes in, what price will you use? Again, many new businesses make that mistake and saddle themselves with low prices they don't feel able to alter.

Our contention is that you should never defend your price. It's the price for the job and altering it after it is declared shows you have a weak position open to negotiation.

The way prices are perceived is interesting. Why is something that cheap? You never see a house that is £205,000. It is either £195,000 or more obviously £199,950. You never see a car that is £4,000. It is always £3,950 or it is £4,200. This is a matter of perception. Almost anything we buy in shops (clothing, toys etc.) isn't a round number, but something more like .99.

Money depreciates in value. Sadly, the days when Pound shops actually meant that everything stocked was £1, have gone.

We've seen some struggling businesses where the answer was to put up the prices and not lower them. Perception alters and the idea that money is a constant measure for value is a flawed one. Why are some training courses priced at £1,500 or more and some others struggle to fill their places at £30?

Buying and Selling a Business

It's useful to consider the price you may get or have to pay for a business. It may be a good idea to set up your business so that it can be sold in a few years. To do that, it must have some features.

Any saleable business must not depend on the expertise or the contacts of the current owner. If that is the case, then the minute they leave, the business will fold also. There must be a customer base that is reliable or quantifiable so that a forward run of expected sales and income can be demonstrated. It must be capable of being run by anyone with a certain level of knowledge in that field. It must be seen to be profitable. Many small businesses make the mistake of dealing in cash and creating a kind of black market where their business is profitable and vibrant but their books show only minimal figures. This is illegal, of course, as it is really only done to evade taxes.

For example, A bought a gardening business from a retiring gardener who had a full customer book. He paid good money for what he thought was a thriving business but when he started to visit the customers, he found that their loyalty was to the retiring gardener and many decided not to have a gardener anymore. The customer list A had bought proved to be worthless.

Cash Payments

Using cash is not illegal, but anything unusual attracts attention. It isn't your business to establish what your supplier does with cash you have paid over, but it is illegal for a supplier to insist you pay cash to avoid VAT, for example. At the point where someone pays cash into a bank, the bank employee at the till is personally liable in law for making enquiries about the unusual transaction, to counter money laundering.

> Beware if you are buying someone else's business – check out its accounts and its customers.

Should I Be Charging VAT?

For practical purposes the "VAT Threshold" exists and is £85,000 (2023). Below this level of turnover in a year, the business need not register for VAT. You may register if below that figure, but you do not have to do so. It is mandatory, however, in the year in which your turnover is expected to rise above that level. You're not supposed to wait for it to reach that figure if it's obviously going to do so.

Setting up costs enjoy a special privilege in that the VAT may be claimed back for once-only set-up costs for up to three years after starting. Otherwise VAT is a rolling commitment to collect from your customers on one hand. After setting it off against any VAT you've paid out to your suppliers, submit the net figure to the HMRC quarterly (usually).

There are two systems of collection and many small businesses use what is called cash accounting which has some advantages. Standard VAT depends on your invoiced amount (hence the phrase "Tax Point" against the date you will see) which may cause you difficulties if you have late or delayed payers. You should always consult a professional if you think you are going to be involved with VAT. In theory you always receive the cash for it before you have to pay out, therefore giving you the use of funds in your bank account for up to three months, but this is subtle and needs to be fully understood.

VAT used to be handled by Customs and Excise but this has now been amalgamated within HMRC. Never try to play tricks with the VAT people. Talk to them quickly about any problems that arise. Any modern accounting system will help handle the VAT cashflow in your business.

TR Limited was a family business supplying model shops as a wholesaler and also running some direct online sales themselves. The accountant rang one day to say there was a problem with VAT and that some £21,000 was owed. This was a big sum to find for them and a cause for worry. We immediately could see that this could not be so. The whole of last year's VAT bill was only £28,000 or around £7,000 per quarter. The accountant calculated again and confirmed the figure. The company imported some goods from America (no VAT there) and some from Europe and some from China and the Far East. A quick rough calculation wasn't possible, therefore, but something was wrong.

Eventually it turned out that the accounting system had accidentally been set to count one month in the quarter for the last two quarters. The calculations were short by two months for each of the two quarters. The amount owed was substantially less than the figure suggested.

Get help with VAT!

Invoicing/Collecting Money

Obviously, you should invoice for what you are owed. But there are some misconceptions about it. See the pricing for some related guidance. You should not give discounts unless there's a good reason.

AF was setting up his new business and decided he would start by giving everyone a thirty per cent discount. On further enquiry he had no particular reason for doing so but believed that was a good thing to do. We dissuaded him.

Your invoices should look as if they belong to you with proper headings and a consistent format. You should incorporate your terms and conditions which should not be a surprise to your customer. Include your bank details and double check to make sure they are correct to save a lot of problems. State clearly on the invoice the date it is due to be paid. Without that, it's difficult to make a claim in a small claims court if the customer doesn't pay.

An invoice isn't a letter. It's normal to send an invoice which is simply a list of work done or reference to a contract or some other detail so that the payer can pin down what they're paying for. There is no need usually to go into a lot of detail.

It should include your company details, a heading, a tax date, a description explaining the work that relates to it and instructions for payment. These days, it's probably a good idea not to give an option for cheques. Just leave it out. If they send you a cheque, all well and good, so long as you allow enough time to be sure the cheque is paid. However, that means you have to physically take it somewhere to pay in. Plus, there's a cost in bank charges for doing so once you've gone past your introductory free period.

> Invoices need to show the work done, how to pay (bank details), date they are due, even if it is immediately, and your logo and other details.

You should have a method of keeping up with what work is chargeable and what items to include. Do not rely on your memory. Make sure your invoices are issued in a timely manner. There's no point in waiting and you should have a diary system for checking and chasing payments.

You hear and see many forms of "Ts and Cs" (Terms and Conditions), bandied about. You can add to it what you want in theory, as long as it's a reasonable thing. If your business is involved and sizeable contracts are in hand, then you should have properly prepared Ts and Cs – better to have them drawn up by a lawyer. If you're dealing in small invoices in a simple way, it's enough to put "Payment on receipt" or "Payment with order" or some phrase that suits your circumstances.

The idea that you should allow thirty days after the end of the month or some other arrangement is nonsense and should be avoided by small businesses. You must consider what you're going to do about delayed payments. Are you going to sue? Probably not, but you might go to the Small Claims Court in a serious case involving several hundred pounds. That will be the end of any commercial arrangements between you, of course, but there's a point where that is both unavoidable and a good thing.

By law, you are entitled to charge interest on late payments and it's worth looking up the details. You can also offer a reduction for prompt payment which may work for your business. That's a simple ploy to encourage payment with no legal implications. For small amounts it's probably of no value that makes any sense.

There are ways of applying pressure if a payment is overdue. Statements are normally associated with banks but essentially, they are the same thing. Your "account" with your trading partner sees transactions coming and going and it can be a useful reminder if you issue a statement which shows payments made and what is outstanding.

There must always be a presumption at first that anything overdue is an oversight. If you suspect not, then work through the civilities quickly. Depending on the level of familiarity, the first thing to do might be an email or a text. "Can I just remind you..." is possibly a good way to start. The second stage might be to send a statement. Various options are open to you and you should not shrink from chasing. A phone call might do the trick or mention it while you are there. "Just popped in to see if I can pick up a cheque from you..." is good pressure but some way down the line.

The way we deal with people and other businesses in the UK is polite and plays on embarrassment. At the same time we can exert considerable pressure without rancour. It's always good to leave the other person with dignity, even if we really do know what is going on. Having said all that, you're entitled to be paid as agreed and should be able to chase where necessary.

Chase your invoices – you are entitled to be paid.

STARTING SOMETHING WITH NOTHING

GT Ltd was a manufacturer of large trailers for articulated lorries. His main customer was a transport company conveniently sited next door. We were approached when he had chronic cash-flow problems. After examining his costs and his pricing we looked at how he was paid. "It's supposed to be sixty days from invoice but they take ninety days usually," was the answer, which is an extraordinary time for any small business to go without payment – especially in a manufacturing case where the costs of materials, premises and the workforce are all stacking up. Calculating the payments made and listing the invoices showed that his customers were not taking ninety days as presumed but actually payments were not banked until one hundred and twenty days (or more) had elapsed. No wonder the business was having cash-flow problems! The owner was scratching around for wages at the end of the week, juggling suppliers to try to keep up and was, in fact, slowly going under.

The next thing was to address the situation. "I can't chase them – if I upset them they are eighty per cent of my business." The smart reply is, well, if you don't, they will have eighty per cent of no busines at all. For any business to be dependent on another to that extent is a major alarm bell ringing. However, at that point, we persuaded the owner to go next door and talk to the boss about outstanding amounts. It's unlikely they will want to lose such a convenient supplier and a friendly relationship existed. The immediate answer was that they had a cheque on reception just waiting to be brought around and because of holidays it had been sitting there for a fortnight!

The underlying problems needed to be sorted out urgently once the immediate needs had received attention. The main problem was the reliance on one customer. This is never a good idea.

The Bank Account

To start with, it isn't unusual to struggle to open a business account with any bank. Some of our clients are finding the newer "challenger" banks are more accommodating.

If you can, choose your bank with an eye to the future. If you develop and need bank help in the future it will be helpful if they can see who you are, what you are and how well you have done. It's helpful if your private accounts are in the same place as your busines accounts. Some people think otherwise but they are not helping their case.

If you are running a company with community involvement, you may want to use a bank that specialises in that sector (like the co-op) or if you are keen on ethical and green issues, there is Triodos Bank. Other than that, there's little to choose between the main banks. They will all offer you a period of free banking. There are some accounts offered with other banks that have advantages for small businesses, but these might not be so good if the business has plans to grow.

Planning Ahead

As a new business, your plans for the future are volatile. As things develop, your focus and your successes may form a recognisable path, enabling a plan to be made with more accuracy. A useful Planning Tool is the Cash Flow Forecast, often requested by lenders. Once understood, it's an invaluable aid to running a business.

There are few businesses that can really run day-to-day without planning. Owners of such businesses will get caught out sooner or later and their lack of management forethought will tell against them in any lending assessment.

A Cash Flow Forecast is normally an Excel spreadsheet which means it adds up for you and any alterations are automatically recalculated. If you use a template already prepared, then don't worry if some of the categories/boxes are not relevant to you. It's better to leave them blank. That does two things: it shows you have considered the point and decided there is nothing and it also keeps intact any underlying formula for calculations.

Keep in mind all throughout the words "reasonable expectancy." People often ask: "How do I know what the money will be in nine months' time?" Using an informed guess, you can easily build up a reasonable picture and it does not matter if it is not exact. The point is it's a plan, drawn up from where you stand right now. Although it looks ahead a year, or maybe three years, it's still a plan which may alter as we proceed through the time involved. The further you look ahead from now, the less likely it is to be exact.

> Cashflows help you plan ahead and see looming problems before they happen. Make one that works for you.

We have seen three and even five-year plans used, but for a small business, it doesn't make much sense to look ahead more than a year or so. A cashflow is just drawing a picture as you see it now for the next year. What you should do is redraw it in, for example, three months' time so that you always have at least a year ahead planned. Your revisions will be with the benefit of new facts and realisations – an education you did not have back at the start.

The spreadsheet works in monthly columns on the basis of money in, minus money out and then what's left. Then it's repeated for the next column. It does not need to be in months but that is usually the most useful measure. You can usefully have subtotals at the end of each section, so that you can compare one month with another.

At the bottom of each column, you have a summary section. This repeats the starting figure (i.e. what was left at the end of the previous month) plus the money that is expected to come in and then the figure for the money going out. The resulting total for what's left is at the bottom, ready to carry that forward as the starting figure for the next monthly column in line. You will see that the "bottom line" is a reflection of what your bank balance will be (if it all goes as planned). The phrase "Bottom Line" comes from this exercise.

As this is a plan, we shall now be able to foresee when we are likely to run out of money! That is very useful.

So, if we have completed the exercise, filling in what money is expected and when, filling in the expenses for the amounts we know about and a reasonable guess for what we don't know, we should have a bottom line that will tell us something useful.

There are only two things you can do about money. You can get more in or you can spend less. Better still, you can usually do a little of each. If your plan runs out of money, then we need to do something. It is better to find this out on paper first.

You must not tell fibs! Using the phrase "reasonable expectancy," can we revise any of our expectations to redraw the picture? Can we delay any of the planned expenditure we obviously can't afford as early as planned? Are there any other funds available or can we increase our activity in some way to generate more income? Ultimately, if it cannot be made to work, then it's better to find out in advance.

Certain figures will remain the same each month but for others the figure may change, depending on the season or some other influence. Christmas sales may be doubled for example. February sales may be low because of the time of year. Heating costs will be more in winter unless you have a budget scheme in place with the supplier. It is important that the figures you put into your plan reflect what can be expected for that month. Don't divide a yearly figure by twelve unless it really does go through the bank monthly.

Don't forget that if you invoice in one month you may not actually get paid for another month. The words "Cash Flow Forecast" are each individually important. It is cash only; it is a forecast and it shows a flow of money. It isn't an accounting exercise, so do not include any book figures (depreciation, allowances for bad debts etc.).

Although we don't know exactly what the figures will be in a year's time, we can build up a picture of how we see it at that moment. We can now plan when we can afford to invest in a piece of equipment or take on some campaign or other. More importantly, we can get it wrong on paper and know what we need to do to avoid some of the pitfalls.

We can also try things out. What if we employ someone in six months' time? Shall we buy that piece of equipment in six months' time? Shall we take on extra office space in a few months' time? You can insert the costs and the ongoing service costs into your forecast and see what damage it does to your bottom line! If it's too much, then you have some options. Obviously, you can delay that expenditure but do consider if that will hold back your development. You might decide that you could go to the bank for a small loan or overdraft.

As with all big purchases you have choices and options. Take some thought over the following to see if they apply:

How sorely do you need that item?

Can you find a cheaper/budget one (that will be good enough)?

Can you borrow one?

Can you share one?

Is it available second-hand?

Can you trade in or sell the old one?

Can you take out a loan?

Can you have it on hire purchase?

Is it available on lease or perhaps on hire?

The point is to lessen the impact on your cash flow.

JK bought a road surface sweeper and set himself up as a sole trader. His idea of going to the docks area found him plenty of work but he didn't realise that the big companies who employed him expected to be invoiced at the end of the month and given at least thirty days to pay. Having invested all his available funds in the machine and equipment, after three weeks he had no more to buy fuel and was effectively stopped until someone paid him. If he had asked some of the questions listed above, he might not have ended up in such a position.

SUMMARY

- Price carefully:
  Cover all your costs.
  People rarely buy the cheapest.

- Invoices:
  Include all the necessary
  info and chase payments
  if they are not made by the
  date you said they were due.

- Be careful if you are buying
  someone else's business –
  check everything they tell you.

- Get help with VAT!

- Cashflow Forecasts need not
  be complicated and help you
  control your money, plan ahead
  and see problems coming.
  Make yours work for you.

STARTING SOMETHING WITH NOTHING

Chapter Nine

The Bits You'd Rather Not Touch
(But Should Know Something About)

Accounting /Bookkeeping/Tax etc.

Many people have a brain fog around anything to do with keeping accounts. The purpose for doing so is quite straightforward and need not instil panic. Like many things, you can complicate it but if you're one who doesn't naturally feel comfortable with figures and admin, it's useful to strip it all right down to its simple basics.

We all have to pay tax. It enables the authorities to keep up the roads and drains, defend us, run the NHS and much more, of course. One reason for keeping records is your tax position. If you are forming a limited company for your business, you as a director will effectively be an employee of the shareholder(s), which may or may not be you. As a director you are allowed to take your salary irregularly depending, for example, on the health of the bank balance and outside the PAYE scheme. Normally any other employee will take a salary or wages regularly through the Government's PAYE scheme. PAYE stands for "Pay As You Earn" and is a way of anticipating your tax position for the year so that the government revenues will come in quicker and more regularly. Very often people get paid regular amounts at regular intervals so the principle is clever and means the country's Exchequer gets income continually and not in annual amounts. It sets up requirements for adjustments, refunds and special allowances which starts to complicate things.

If you're a shareholder, you can get some money from your company as a dividend, which is taxed at a lower rate than income tax and does mean money is coming to you without National Insurance (NIC) payments as well. You are only allowed to draw dividends from profit though, but whereas most share investments pay dividends once or twice a year typically, there is no particular requirement to do that. As long as there is profit in the company bank balance, it can be distributed to the shareholders. It means that all shareholders get paid a dividend — regardless of whether they've actually done any work or not — whereas salary/wages are usually related to particular work being done. The HMRC take a dim view of anyone whose working income is solely through dividends from their own company.

It's useful to understand all that, because in a business where someone has only contributed money, yet does little otherwise and the director does all the work but had no money to put toward the business, the director can get paid for what they do. Then, only when profits are made, does the shareholder get reward. Later on we will expound more on the topic of companies.

> Company directors can pay themselves a salary which is subject to PAYE and if they own the company too, they can also pay themselves a "dividend" from the company's profits.

Accounting allows all this to be "accounted for." If you have a little business where it's only you, then you are a "sole trader" or if there is more than one of you in the business, you can be a partnership. A partnership is an "unincorporated body" and is more than just two sole traders working together. If it's a business partnership, then each partner can commit the business to an expenditure. If that was not the case, then no one would be able to trade with the business and trust that the business was trading properly. Similarly, with an incorporated limited company, the director is deemed to have all the company's rules properly established and complied with, unless there's reason to believe otherwise. If that was not the case, no one would be able to trade with that company.

The tax position that results from either sole trading or partnership is different to a company and a company director. Each of us, regardless of working state, has a liability for tax. This is drawn from any yearly income you receive from any or whatever source. This is your pot of income, so to speak. You may have income from a job, or several jobs, savings or investments, a pension, the profit made from selling a major asset, income from rents or anything else making up your pot for this year. In theory, that would include all that is added up. You are subject to the rules on tax, but there are allowances that reduce your liability.

> Sole traders are self-employed and must pay tax at the end of the year based on their earnings from the business after all the costs have been deducted.

Everyone is allowed to earn up to the basic "personal allowance" and pay no tax on that. It is set by the government each year to run from April to April. This is the "Tax Year" for historical reasons. You can look this up, but it is around £12,000. Above that you pay basic rate tax on your income until you earn more than a certain amount (around £44,000). You pay a higher rate after that.

There are other allowances that may apply. Your main residence is exempt, so if you sell that at a profit, there is no income or capital gains tax to pay. Other properties or assets sold at a profit have an allowance that applies there too, but otherwise tax is due. PAYE deals with any normal employment, even where multiple jobs are involved. It also deals with pensions and some other regular income. This leaves the profit you may get from your business. We shall not know what that is until the end of the year.

This is where accounting/bookkeeping comes into play. Your profit is calculated after you have made a list of your sales and taken off a list of all the expenditure that enabled that to happen. There are other allowances you may be able to deduct (for example, for working from home and the costs associated with that). Depreciation is another "book entry," which is a calculation based upon allowing yearly for the cost of the renewal of a piece of equipment after its life expired. However, mostly it's money that you have actually paid out.

So we need some lists – money earned and money spent. There is no legal reason why you should do this as you go along, but you need to do so sometime to arrive at the figures for the year. It's better to do it as you go along, so that you don't forget anything, and so that you can see how you are doing. For example, by drawing a line every month and totting up your lists, you can see if the business is doing enough or not enough.

Keep all receipts. It's possibly every accountant's nightmare for someone to dump a pile of receipts on them once a year, so keep a summary every month. You should be able to tie up the bank balance with what you have had coming in and what has gone out.

> Keep Lists.

Keep lists of everything you spend on the business and all your income. Keep receipts and copies of invoices.

On a simple basis, that is what is required. You don't have to do any of it on a computer. It can be manual, though the tax return you have to do yearly is computer-based nowadays. It's probably better to do it on the computer. You do not necessarily have to employ a bookkeeper or accountant but it is usually better to do so. They understand and have everyday knowledge of the allowances and what you can do to your best advantage.

Some computer-based systems are designed with the small business in mind (and the accountant's sanity): QuickBooks is popular, as is Xero, with SAGE being a more complex system for bigger businesses. There are others. The best thing to do is talk to your accountant and find out what they recommend. That means you are using the system they like to use which is better for everyone. Help your accountant to help you. It'll be cheaper and probably better.

The computer systems have other advantages. They enable you to issue invoices, to show you lists and calculate things automatically. However, all computer systems are only as good as the data you feed in.

If you have a turnover that is higher than the VAT threshold, you will certainly need computer assistance. Those systems calculate what you owe. The VAT threshold is set annually by the government and is the level of turnover beneath which you do not necessarily have to register and collect VAT for the Government. It also means you can't claim VAT back. Talk to your accountant about the implications of the different systems for collecting and paying over VAT. In any case, if your turnover (which is the amount of money you take in for your business activities or, in some cases, the amount you invoice for) breaches that level or is clearly going to breach that threshold in that specific trading year, you are obliged to register and implement the VAT requirements.

Don't have a business with a turnover just above the threshold – keep it below or aim to go well above it. The amount of work involved is considerable. If you have held out in a growing business and you eventually have to register for VAT, the impact on your pricing needs to be planned in advance. In most cases you will need to add twenty per cent (currently) on your prices for VAT. Either your prices will be seen to have increased or your business will take in that substantial cost. The marketing implications need to be thought through.

Companies, Sole Traders, Partnerships, and the Legal Stuff

Be careful when a lot of people talk about their "company," yet it isn't a legally formed company. Largely through ignorance the terms used for company, firm and partnership are muddied in many people's minds.

> Sole traders are self-employed and must pay tax at the end of the year based on their earnings from the business after all the costs have been deducted.

Firms

A Sole Trader is one person set up in business. They are completely liable for anything they do and whatever profit is made is theirs to keep after tax is paid. There may be a business/trading name. This means that the individual is still liable for any loans or debts of the business, even if the business fails.

A Partnership is any number of people banded together in a business. Each is capable of committing the business to an expense and each is liable for their own tax position. Unless there's written agreement, the partners share the profits between them in varying ways. They also share the liabilities; that means each partner is liable for loans and debts of the business, even if the business ceases. Usually they have a business name.

These are all called firms which means that they are in business, but are not incorporated officially as a company. It makes sense to have a "Partnership Agreement" drawn up while everyone is still friends and which sets out the agreed ownership rules for the business and what happens if any one partner leaves.

Limited Companies

A Company is an incorporated business, which means it has been registered at Companies House (with a few exceptions) under a Memorandum and Articles of Association. The M&As is basically the constitution of the company including the make-up of shareholdings, what the company is for and all the rules it needs to follow.

Mostly standard M&As are used for ease and cheapness, but technically that isn't necessary. Companies are set up in accordance with the various Companies Acts as they apply.

Shareholders are the owners of the company. The directors are the ones who run the company from day-to-day and may or may not include some shareholders. In your small company, if you appoint yourself as a director you are in effect your own employee! There are various legal responsibilities attached to a director's role, regardless of whether or not they are the owners (i.e. the shareholders). It basically comes down to behaving yourself and making sure you keep the company's affairs in good order.

There are some key reasons for forming a company. One is legal protection. A company is a "separate legal entity." Its activities are only to do with you in so far as you are a shareholder or a director. The "Limited" bit is that the owners have limited liabilities. That "Ltd" you see alongside the company's name is actually a warning to all who trade with the company, that the owners are not personally liable for the debts of the company (unless you have taken steps to get around this in some way).

There have been some very high-profile cases over the years when a company has "gone to the wall" (when a company loses all its money and ultimately fails) as the expression goes, but the owners and directors can let it go without personally being liable (If they are liable, it's because someone has made them give a guarantee of some kind backed up with assets.). Unfortunately, this also means that sometimes you can see unscrupulous folk who have lost a business, owing money all round, only to set up a similar business the next week to carry on.

Once the business debts of the company are paid in a particular year – which may include salary for the director(s) – then the profits belong to the shareholders, in accordance with the number of shares they own. On an ongoing business, the profits may be distributed to the shareholders as a dividend on their shares. This was mentioned elsewhere. Dividends are income, but not in the same way that a salary is income. Dividends have better tax arrangements. You can only have a dividend, however, if profits have been made and if all the shareholders receive their allocations. The directors run the company and, of course, they need to retain some money in the business to finance the next year's round of trading. Therefore, not all the profits will be distributed.

The second reason for forming a company is simply that tax positions can be advantageous if handled well. A company's tax year isn't necessarily the same as a personal one and undistributed profits may happily remain in the company until it is convenient to draw them off. This means that owners might not wish to draw income in one tax year when it is advantageous to do so in another. Various amounts can be written off against tax liabilities for a company that doesn't exist for personal ownership. The possibilities of contributions to a pension scheme also may be useful. There is nothing wrong with reasonable tax avoidance. Tax evasion is illegal. There is a distinction.

> Sole traders and partnerships are independent and save the costs associated with running a company, but do not have the protection of limited liability, Companies have to follow more rules, may have shareholders to answer to, but have the benefit of limited liability and sometimes, tax benefits too.

Other Types of Company

What we have described so far is a normal trading company. There are other types. The three main ones are those used by charities and social enterprises – companies limited by guarantee, CIOs (charitably incorporated organisations) and CICs (community interest companies). They all have the benefits of limited liability, but have no shareholders to facilitate a not-for-profit, more co-operative way of running.

If a not-for-profit company is required and the intention is to register as a charity, then a company limited by guarantee is often the best choice. The difference is that instead of shareholders, trustees are appointed to a board. There are still directors and there will still be profits, otherwise the company won't be around very long! However, the profits are not distributed to shareholders as the company doesn't have any. The profits are all retained in the company for the benefit of the work that it's doing. The trustees are responsible for the company to the extent of their guarantee. That is often £10, but can be any amount. In most other respects, the company operates as it would as an ordinary trading company.

This is not an exhaustive list. There are other forms of ownership available but less common and more specialised in use.

Companies House

Companies House is where all limited and other types of incorporated business must be registered and various things need to be submitted to them annually or as they happen on a regular basis (accounts, annual returns, changes in ownership, changes in directors, changes in location etc.).

The register is a useful thing to check when you are naming your business — even if it isn't a limited company. You can enter the name you are thinking of using and Companies House will tell you if that name is available. If someone else already has that name, you can't use it. If you do, you could be guilty of "passing off" (pretending to be that other company with the same name).

The same principle applies if you are not registered as a company. If there can be any confusion about you being the same as another business, it can be challenged and you can be forced to change your name. The problem works the other way round. Once you have worked hard to establish your name and reputation, you would not want someone else taking your customers due to misunderstanding. Plus, you have no control over their actions and they could bring your business into disrepute.

A simple way to check is to do an internet search on your proposed name and see if anyone in your area has the same business name. There's no longer a formal register of business names apart from Companies House for incorporated companies. There is a commercial company offering protection for your business name if registered with them. The fees allow them to defend your name if it is challenged or if you wish to challenge anyone else.

As discussed elsewhere, it's ideal if you can co-ordinate your company/business name with your domain name/web address, your email address, your Twitter handle and how you label yourself anywhere else.

Leases and Property

If your business is going to operate from your house, you need to check whether you need any sort of planning permission or any sort of inspection of the premises (particularly for food-related businesses). If your house is rented, you need to check whether you require the landlord's permission.

If you're taking on the lease of a premises, check this carefully (or get an expert if you can afford one):

- Who is responsible for maintenance and who pays for it?
- Can you make internal changes?
- What is included in the rent (e.g. electricity, water and/or council tax)?
- How long are you (and the landlord) committed for and is that what you want? Short-term leases are good if you aren't sure about the location for the business, but it is precarious and the landlord could ask you to leave when you don't want to. Long-term leases are more secure, but then you are committed to pay the rent whether you want to stay or not.
- Is the person you're dealing with the actual landlord? If not, does he have the right to sub-let?
- Usually, the landlord is responsible for all things to do with the building and property (in other words the facility allowing you to trade) and the tenant is responsible for furniture, moveable fittings, the bills for utilities and anything to do with actually using the property.
- Are you required to pay VAT on the rent? That is for the landlord to say and can be either way.
- Make sure you see the insurance for the building every year.

There is no such thing as a "standard lease." A lease is simply an agreement between two or more parties – a contract. There can be anything in a lease so long as it is commercially reasonable. Therefore, make sure you check before signing anything. You must understand what you are signing for. There is no legal obligation for either party to use a solicitor to act, but it is very advisable and an expense that can save you from a bad situation later.

A young couple took on the lease of a building to open a restaurant. They spent all their savings refurbishing the interior but a day or so before they were due to open, a repossession order arrived in the post, addressed to their landlord. They attended the court proceedings, saying that they had a valid lease with the landlord and could not be made to leave. The judge was sympathetic, but the landlord didn't have the authority to sublet so their lease turned out to be worthless and they lost everything (There's a happy ending to this story: We found a local solicitor who gave them pro bono help and they successfully took action against the landlord's solicitors who had advised them on the lease. They won all the money they had invested back, but it took two or three years.).

SD was going into business for the first time as a "back street garage." He arranged a lease with the owner of a rundown set of buildings behind the station. His part was to be a set of sheds and a building in the middle of this so-called industrial estate. In fact, the lease included only the footprint of the building in the middle of these properties with no provision for parking or even access, should the landlord wish to be difficult at any stage. This wasn't ideal for a garage business with half a dozen customers requiring vehicular access every day. Luckily, we were able to help him get his lease re-drawn with the required permissions in place.

A company was going to be established as a community business to take over a small leisure centre from the local council who was losing money annually and not running it well. A feasibility study was done and there were many ways the business could be run and developed sensibly to relieve the council of its problem. Unfortunately, the council insisted that, though the lease for the footprint of the buildings could be a ten-year lease, the playing fields could only be a three-year lease. This meant that the playing fields could be sold off by the council at some point leaving a leisure centre with no outdoor facilities. In any case, the car park needed to be included with the buildings, but to be able to raise funds as a charitable concern, the company would need a lease that was at least twenty one years for the whole property. The council legal department couldn't see that their terms were completely unattainable, yet they insisted that the terms were acceptable.

Insurance

Every business MUST have insurance (public liability as a minimum, employer's liability if you employ people or use volunteers and product liability if you make something to sell) with other more specialised forms for particular industries. There are many good insurance companies and brokers around who will advise you on what you need and give you competitive prices. Do not scrimp on the insurance values, because in the event of a claim, if it is established that you insured at half the replacement value to keep the premiums down, then you will only get half of whatever claim you are making. Even if your claim isn't total loss and only a part of the insured property, you will only get half of its value. This is called averaging.

You may need licences or testing in some cases. Producing cosmetic creams or skin products for example, need to have independent testing. Food production is subject to approval from environmental authorities. A restaurant or café has to display their star rating for food hygiene. If you sell alcohol, you need a licence from magistrates. Particular insurance is required if you are carrying out any sort of risky operation (using ladders for example). A cleaning company needs to be aware of COSHH regulations. The list goes on and on.

It's a good idea if you can spend some time working for someone in the industry or sector in which you wish to start your business. Starting with no experience at all is a bad idea.

SUMMARY

- Pick the type of business which fits with you.
- Sole traders and partnerships can become companies at a later date.
- Check out your company name before you commit to it.
- Keep books – even if they are just simple lists of money earned and spent.off.
- Get help with tax.
- Be careful with leases.
- You must have insurance.

BOB SHEPHERD & KAREN DAVIES

STARTING SOMETHING WITH NOTHING

Chapter Ten
Following Your Nose

Running your business starts with a good plan, but it's often supplemented by the need to improvise!

Business Plans

Everybody needs a business plan, but nobody wants one! This is because a business plan has become a thing that the bank asks for. It's written because it's asked for to borrow money or get a grant. We have heard people say, "that's written for the bank" or stating, without any understanding at all, "I have got a business plan; it's in a drawer somewhere and I've never looked at it!"

The clue to all this is in the words of the title. It is a PLAN for the business and it is about the proposed BUSINESS. A year or two back the banking industry was saying that they were rarely seeing good business propositions from small businesses. Research published about the same time established that most small businesses were not even bothering to approach banks because they thought they would be refused anyway. Which was the chicken and which was the egg?

Both the huge rise of alternative finance options for business on one hand and the attitude of the banks on the other have moved them away from being the go-to lenders to the business community that was once the case.

A business plan is a working document: it needs to be useful. It's an observation at one point looking ahead. As such, it needs revision in the light of experience and further education (it's a plan, after all.).

What is the purpose of your business plan?

- It is a summary of what is intended, the resources required and how it is going to work.
- It enables the business owner to marshal their thoughts and resources.
- It can show off to someone else that you know what you are talking about.

Each plan is different because every business is different. A template is probably a silly idea. There are some common features and usual ways of considering what is necessary, because that often makes sense. If you do use a template, make sure you butcher it and make it your own.

When you are especially presenting your ideas to someone else (for money perhaps), you need to show that it is your plan and not someone else's. Many templates come in the form of a list of questions that you are supposed to answer. If the question is relevant, then answer it. Do this fully and not with just a one-word answer. Afterwards, delete the question and insert a suitable heading.

A list of possible headings appears below. These aren't definitive and need to be cut to fit. If the plan is for your own use only, then you do not necessarily need to spell out all the legalities and who owns what. You do need to consider everything though it might make more sense to make a series of lists, detailing maybe what is needed, where you will get it from and how these things are going to be applied.

Every plan seems to start with an executive summary. Who it was who came up with this idea is lost in the mists of time. If you are presenting it to someone else then it's a good idea to have an *Introduction* that sets out the general idea. There is nothing executive about that. If it's for your own use, then you can happily dispense with it. It may also be a good idea to finish up with a *Conclusion* and if you're requesting finance, it's good to add a summary of what finance is required, over what period and a summary of how you are going to pay it back under what terms etc. This shows you have ownership of the whole proposition and are not floundering around in the dark.

Don't forget that anything you write is to be received by someone else. You can't assume they know anything. They may be visual thinkers, so include sensible illustrations. They may be list-oriented procedural thinkers, so include summaries with bullet points where there's a block of text. They may be number people, so be clear about your numbers and make sure they are the same all the way through.

A very small one-man band business will not need all the detail listed below but the essence of it is still there regardless of the size. A formal business plan for a small business requiring funding might have the following headings and contents:

Title page: Include address and contact numbers and any disclaimers.

Contents page: If you must. Keep in mind, however, that this is a business document; not a book.

Introduction: Do not go into detail. That is for later. Set out the idea, why the owners think it's a good idea and some indication of how big this is. Draw a verbal picture. Do not be tempted to be too enthusiastic. You believe in the project, but they don't yet. Do not make sweeping statements assuming the whole world must think as you do.

Legal basis/Formation details: Explain briefly the basis of the company or firm. Supporting documents can be in the appendix.

Those involved/Key people: List the main people running it or involved in some way. Give a short "thumbnail sketch" in a few lines including experience, role, responsibilities etc. (Small head shots?). CVs can be included in the appendix if you think they add something. If you do, say so. External people may be involved; solicitors or accountants perhaps.

Premises: What do you need to do or what have you arranged? For how long? On what terms? etc. Where is it? Are there any advantages? Add descriptions of facilities if relevant. Picture?

Equipment: Summarise it if it's complicated. Explain what is needed and what you have.

The Market (and what you are going to do about it): Explain clearly what you are doing initially to get going, who you are involving and how your campaign is going to develop. Include perhaps a couple of pictures of what you are producing. More can go in the appendix.

Process: You may need to talk about your suppliers; your production process maybe. How many people do you need? This is where you introduce money into the plan because you need to explain the whole business from the beginning to when you get paid and on round again. If there's no production process as such, the cycle is still there. In a very small business you may need to explain how you are going to feed yourself for the first few months.

Finances: What you have, what you need and how you are hoping to get it (never presume – it's better to ask nicely). If there's a lot to say, then consider a table for clarity. Consider if you need to have calculations for break even. When will you make a profit? What about follow-up finance? At this point, you should say if you might need help later.

Cash Flow Forecast: Introduce and summarise what your Cash Flow Forecast tells you. List any assumptions made about growth, expansion or seasonality.

SWOT analysis: A favourite item in the business plans. It stands for Strengths and Weaknesses; Opportunities and Threats. Tabulate these sensibly (remembering what you have already said). Be honest and realistic and put away your rose-tinted spectacles.

Conclusion: Give an honest appraisal of the main points. It's your last chance to sell it and show ownership and belief/confidence. Having prepared the plan above, you should have the conclusion by now.

Appendices:

Cash Flow Forecasts

Provisional Profit and Loss

Survival Requirements

Any other financial lists – setting up costs, for example.

CVs

Marketing Materials

Photographs

Any other supporting documents.

You should aim at between ten to twenty pages for the main plan. If it's bigger than that, you are either not a small business or you have waffled on too much. Your CVs should be one page, ideally. Your appendices can take up as many pages as is sensible to add detail to your plan.

Remember the whole should show you have a good business idea, that you are the one(s) to carry it through and that you have a good idea of what you are intending to do; how, why and when. You should also show a good grasp of what you might do if it does not go to plan (contingencies).

In spite of all your careful planning, one thing is almost certain: Things won't follow the plan in the way you thought they would. When this happens, DON'T PANIC! A plan is a plan. It's important, but it should remain flexible to any influence. There is plenty that can happen to derail the best plans.

Responding to Disasters and Things not Going to Plan

Nothing goes quite according to plan. That is not why we plan for things. Looking ahead though, gives us the chance to lessen the impact of anything unfortunate. Although many businesses do have a disaster plan in place, for smaller businesses it may only be necessary to keep some options available by sensible caution and provision. The essential thing is that your business can carry on.

One of the most common things to happen is that the rush of customers you anticipated when you started or the firm orders you thought you had, evaporate. If this happens, you just need to re-think your marketing approach. Try some different avenues and keep on trying until the customers build up again.

There could be other disasters. For example, suppose your laptop dies on you. The first question anyone will ask is to find out if it is backed up anywhere. There are various options for that.

What will you do if your van/car breaks down? To have it fixed is the obvious answer but what about your visits and calls for the day? Will you have all the phone numbers you need to make calls from the roadside to say you're going to be delayed or to rearrange for another time? One example of this caught someone out and it was nothing to do with him. An unfortunate accident on the motorway resulted in closure for eight hours, during which time he was stuck, unable to move.

If you're going to give a lecture or a talk somewhere involving slides and a presentation, make sure you have enough with you to do without the technology in the event of a power failure or cable failure or anything interrupting what you're supposed to be doing. Have some handouts or some alternative materials so that it's not a complete write-off and you come away with extra points for managing in adversity!

Making reasonable provision to "do it another way" is always sensible. The point is to remain flexible and open to variation. What could possibly go wrong?

Standard wisdom is to have copies of anything essential to the business maintained at another site in case of premises disasters. These days a lot of that might be circumvented by use of cloud-based records.

Contingency planning is more a state of mind for a small business. Having some appointments "out on the road" inevitably results in a late cancellation sooner or later and you can bet it will be the middle one that is cancelled, leaving you with not enough time to get back to your office or to go home before your next one. Having the ability to work in the intervening period is a bonus made easier by today's technology.

On a simple basis, having your emails coming to your mobile phone is a good idea and easily arranged. Not that you need to be on call twenty-four hours a day.

BG set up a TV aerial business. He dealt with aerials on roofs as well as installations of satellite dishes and associated technology services. As such, he needed a substantial amount of equipment available (ladders and spares) and was on the road every day making his calls. His landline phone number diverted to his mobile number during the day but, of course, he was finding it impossible to answer it at times so had an answerphone, of course. By the end of his day, he was having to deal with forty or fifty messages; some of which required urgent response and messed up his plans for the next day's jobs.

Our suggestion was a simple matter of disciplined approach. Stopping for a tea break mid-morning and mid-afternoon was possible (he didn't always do that) and of course a break for lunch meant that he had time sitting safely in his van several times a day. Of course, he needed his break but extending it by quarter of an hour each time and managing his appointments around that so he allocated that time to making and returning calls, meant he could deal with his day in four sections instead of one big lump of out-of-control demands. It also meant he could respond to local emergencies without doubling up his journey times.

That coupled with a more organised response to calls (see elsewhere – always err on the positive response: "Can you do something today?" "I have a gap in the diary on Thursday when I am on my way past your location so I can come to you then" is so much better) put some control of BG's diary back in his hands and left him feeling less stressed about it all.

Contingencies get more involved and complicated when you have others in your team to organise and employ. Never panic. There will be an answer and especially if you have managed your customers' expectations well so that they are expecting you to deliver the goods but are on your side if you can't.

The Covid Virus lockdowns are an excellent example of something going wrong on a grand scale. Many businesses and a lot of small businesses couldn't do any work or trade for months. The best ones found some other way of doing some form of business – either by delivering online or by adapting to something that was allowed but not part of the previous offerings.

In the first of the lockdowns, a Public House in Caldicot responded by setting up a small protected area outside one of its windows into the car park and becoming a "corner shop" by stocking a lot of foods and domestic goods to sell through the window at good prices. It kept everyone busy, kept the location in mind for local people and offered an alternative to the supermarket down the road. It needed a little simple advertising locally and they were up and running within a week.

> Nothing goes to plan – don't panic.
> Have back-up plans and be ready
> to make them on the hoof.

Expanding Your Business

Suppose you are successful. Suppose you can't manage; having started on your own. It's a better problem to have than having no business at all. Managing expectations is your initial response so that you are not letting down your customers and getting a poor reputation for service.

What you do next depends on the extent of your demand. A small craft business opened, selling handmade bags and other similar goods. They had a good website built. Unfortunately, they found that when the website was live they were receiving orders for small quantities from around the world. The postage for safe delivery, let alone all the different requirements, meant that some goods were being sold at a loss where multiple orders were being received. Single items for private customers were fine but orders for a dozen bags from a seller in Texas for stock in his retail outlet made no sense. The quantity was not enough for a pallet and too large for the post. The prices of the goods were outweighed by the cost of transport and to hold them down used up any profit and more.

The immediate answer was to alter the website so that it clearly meant for UK only and look at the prices for wholesale as well as for retail. It changed the whole offering.

Always keep in mind that TIME is your biggest resource. It may not feel like it at first and there are a lot of messages out there suggesting otherwise. Time is there to be harvested, abused, rationalised, wasted and invested.

MW was a copywriter. She was energetic and industrious and she had a lot of contacts from some years in a career as a successful journalist. In her networking, she had an offer that was appealing and engaging. The work didn't take long and it acted as an introduction, leading to further introductions and more work. Fast forward several months and the offer had become so successful MW was run off her feet. In a rare, quiet moment, MW realised that her offer was using up a lot of her time for very little income. It was time for a change.

In many cases, expanded demand means extra staff needed. The easiest thing to delegate at first will be the administration (or at least some of it), leaving the specialised technical stuff as it is. Rather than employ someone part-time, you might consider a VA. That stands for "virtual assistant." They can act for you in small amounts daily or as required and you normally only pay for the hours used. The hourly rate will be more than you would pay for a direct employee but in many cases you usually get accomplished expertise who can sweep up behind you very well.

Here are some examples of the sort of thing a VA might do for your business, leaving you time and availability to get on with the job:

- Receive calls;
- Book appointments;
- Send out invoices;
- Manage databases and customer records;
- Sales calls (maybe more specialised operators).

Picking Customers Carefully

At first, most small businesses are happy to take on anything that pays. There comes a point where 'Yes, we can do that for you!' is the wrong answer, taking up time and resources for insufficient reward. How you manage this depends upon the sort of work you do and how quickly it grows.

A business needs to grow. It needs to maintain its proportions, so that no one activity outstrips the rest and the background workings are still fit for purpose. It's a difficult thing to achieve. Over-dependence on one customer's work is to be avoided.

RS and TP set up a business involved with data systems, supplanting the old clipboards and manual records with a handheld recording system that would coordinate all the functions quickly and speed up delivery at a fraction of the cost. They were picked up by a fast-growing Facilities Management company that handled premises cleaning and repairs for large multi-site companies. They grew and managed to service all the requirements of their customers. Unfortunately, in doing so they neglected the development of their own business, mostly through lack of time available and when their customer was attracted by a cheaper (but less able) system instead they had nothing to fall back on. Faced with effectively starting again, their position was mentally a challenge as well. They had the technology developed for such a system but no systems for promoting it.

TH was a software designer working under freelance contracts with a big Utility Company. He knew how the company could turn their systems on their head to create an effective automated supply chain for the servicing of all their equipment out in the field. The huge existing systems were all developed piece-meal from the old paper-based reporting and ordering systems and were cumbersome, inflexible and management heavy. His new system would sweep away most of it saving huge amounts of money and increasing effectiveness all round. He could not get acceptance of his ideas from directors who would have had to hand over their trust to him for a complete makeover. Trying to adapt the system for others took him away from the one major Utility Company but was less satisfactory, in that he did not know the companies so well.

The small business owner needs to accept that he can operate better in low numbers and small contracts. This is a cultural problem for anyone who has broken away from the large corporate world to "go it alone."

Spreading the risk, applies to everything in this concept. Not just the payments, but the suppliers, maintaining the workforce, keeping up with the local market and more still.

Checking Potential Customers Before Engagement

There are two points of view for the small business. It depends on the sort of business you are conducting and the prices involved. If you are a small business producing or selling goods for relatively small amounts through one of the online platforms, you can rely on the sales site for guarantees etc.

"eBay" does this particularly well as an intermediary. In any case, you have helpful feedback ratings to look at.

If you are dealing with cash, perhaps as a market trader, then there are only a few things to look out for.

A consultancy dealing in relatively small payments where only your time is involved may take a view and rely on the strength of the relationship you establish. In any case you will only have lost time if the contract goes bad.

Small jobbing activities should rely on a spread of contracts and small jobs rather than seeking the one big project – see reference to this elsewhere.

For anything else you should look into your client before engaging to any great extent. It is worth having an engagement contract or an engagement letter, setting out your understanding from the start. "Extras" are then not a matter for dispute, seeing as you have an understanding signed by you and your customer from the beginning.

For sales of goods, you will have an order and a consignment note/invoice to give you an audit trail that can be referred back to in the event of any query.

You can look into your potential customers in a variety of ways. Do some searches online to see that they have a history that corresponds with your understanding. These days, the internet and social media are invaluable. Do a general search for the name(s) plus a location perhaps, or an activity. Check LinkedIn for companies and people, check Facebook and Twitter ("X") for other clues and check your search engine for news sites, directories and general feedback. Take a view on what you see. Mischievous posts by disgruntled customers or even employees are not unknown. Do not be afraid to mention what you find and see what reaction you get.

Rely on your instinct. The little discords and reservations will add up.

Frauds and Scams

PS was a consultant asked to engage with JW for a new business and planning support. The initial call was followed up by a meeting arranged by the customer at a five-star hotel. It all went well and the right sort of things were said, illustrating a business profile at a high level. Initial payment was made, though for reasons with an explanation they were made through a friend's account (first discord!). However, the money was received so the case proceeded. More meetings followed with emails back and forth; business plans and other material under discussion.

A lot of work was called for but payment had been made and the second payment was made, though a little overdue (second discord). At about this time a phone call with a query was followed up by an email from a different email address to normal but incorporating a name with the same first name. The explanation was that one of the team had used their own personal email and should have used the company one (third discord). Attendance at an exhibition where introductions by PS to business angels for investment was next and the customer turned up in a fourteen-year-old beaten-up car (fourth discord — remember the posh hotel and the high-level working business profile). Delays and excuses about payment prompted PS to follow up with personal enquiries online.

Using 192.com no record of the customer's surname appeared in the town he was living supposedly. No record online of the name came up on a search. Remembering the strange email another search was done using the other surname. An image search was done as well and bingo! News coverage of a £35k VAT fraud conviction was there with a three-year jail sentence given and – crucially – picture evidence that confirmed the customer was indeed the fraudster.

He was trying to use the reputation of PS to gain introductions to money investors hoping they'd ignore the lack of personal investment in the face of a good idea. Subsequent pursuit of the customer through the Small Claims Court for £1,800 of unpaid fees was abandoned when further searches showed he had no assets apart from a winning smile.

Another case involved an accountant, working from home who appeared with a new business plan also wanting introductions for new small businesses. JFG had a string of letters after his name and clearly knew his way around a balance sheet. Two meetings appeared to go well. He wanted to apply for a Local Authority Grant towards new offices. On the third meeting he appeared in a scruffy track suit top and trousers and looked as if he had just been for a run (he hadn't!) (first discord – not what you would expect from an accountant of some standing). He failed to deliver a couple of requirements (second discord) and this prompted a search on his qualifications. Not one institute had heard of him and some of the letters were made up combinations. He was reported to trading standards and was convicted, receiving three years for misrepresentation. A few quick phone calls to the clients that had been introduced recovered the position with no real damage done.

By law you are protected against people misusing your data and the laws dealing with misrepresentation.

Unfortunately, we live in a world where the unwary can get caught out easily. A few simple rules will help in most situations.

- Never give personal information to phone callers, unless you are sure you know who is asking.

- Never give bank or financial details to anyone asking in an unsolicited call or approach.

- Never give out passwords or access details.

- Ensure your passwords are sufficiently obscure to avoid hackers. Use part of an old address or a car numberplate you no longer own or some other obscure thing that you happen to know but which has no link to you now. For sensitive online dealing, such as online banking, for example, make sure you use passwords that are unique to that facility. We need passwords and computer sign-ons for hundreds of things these days and it is very tempting to use a generic password, simply to keep up with quantity required. Don't forget a clever hacker will get a lot of information inadvertently given out about you from studying your social media accounts.

- For bigger contracts, get a memorandum of understanding or Letters of Engagement signed before starting work. It will make you appear more professional anyway.

There is no need to assume everyone you deal with has some criminal intent, but sensible precautions will look professional and will save arguments later.

Other frauds are perpetuated daily and again. It is best not to become too paranoid, but you may want to watch out for:

- Forged Notes: Money is legal tender and although less often used these days it is as well to just bear in mind that a lot of it is circulating still. If you deal in cash regularly take a moment to examine some genuine notes carefully and you will see that it is very difficult to reproduce perfectly. There will be something not quite right about a forged note; the printing quality, the feel of the note perhaps.

- Identity Fraud: Along with other forms of scam, these things are often online these days, because it's easier to be anonymous.

- The attractive deal: The old adage that if it looks too good, beware, holds fast here. We have all won an i-Pad or a million pounds or had an email from some foreign person promising endless riches if we can just pay out a small sum to enable it to happen.

- Online video: Having a Zoom call or some other conference call is fine, unless you have sensitive details lying around in the background.

- Internet access: Passwords again! In one office everyone regularly used several of the computers freely, so the sign-ins and password were attached with a post-it sticker to the side of the computer. The office windows were visible from a public car park area that ran alongside.

Controlling Growth Successfully

It's quite all right if you do not want your business to grow! There could be a number of perfectly valid reasons for keeping it small and sweet. In our modern world there is a presumption that everyone has to be ambitious, want development, progress, growth, increased wealth and all that goes with it.

An intelligent pause for a moment will give light to many reasons why this is not always so and how damaging it can be.

Let us assume that you do want to develop your business. The first thing to repeat is that it must grow all together. Each component part must be in proportion with the company for growth to be successful. If a sudden rush of sales comes in but you do not have the structure to deal with it then the customers will be let down.

Only when all parts of the business structure are working together well can the business thrive and become greater. That is easier to see in a small business, yet a bigger business has more capacity to direct its resources. It's useful to try to imagine exactly what the business needs to look like when it has grown, in maybe a year or two. The Cash Flow Forecast is a useful tool for imagining how that will be financed.

Remember the components of your company that go to make up the structure behind what you are doing. Premises, equipment and "assets"; the admin function, the book-keeping and accounting functions, the people, the financing and the cash circle, the "shouting to the outside world" department — all these need to grow in order for your business to grow. They still need to function when the business is bigger.

Will your premises be adequate still? Do you need better or more equipment? Do you need to engage staff to keep the back office running? Do you need to "up your game" with the promotional activities? Will you need investment to carry out your plans? Notice that whichever division you consider has implications for the rest of it. If you can see that, then you have a structure that is working!

A manufacturing business is the easiest to see how this all works, remembering always that the principles apply completely with every business. It's only the labels and the degree of involvement that changes.

In a manufacturing process, once it has been set up the cycle might start with obtaining the raw materials. Sometimes obtaining more volume will make things easier. The question of delivery may kick in — one of the reasons why large industry uses "Just in Time" delivery of raw materials is to keep the flow going and to iron out the storage problems they would have otherwise. The finance has to be available to pay for those raw materials though usually, unless you are buying small amounts only, terms can be agreed with the supplier, giving time to use the goods and produce an income by selling the result.

So the raw material arrives. Do we have room to store it ready for use? If we do the control of the stock needs to be in place so we re-order in time, and if it has a shelf life then we must use it in order and by certain dates to remain useful.

Using the raw materials usually needs machinery and perhaps a production line. Do we have capacity to cope with the new volumes? Do we need more people? What about increased packaging and transport costs? Will there be more cast-off material to dispose of somewhere? If so, how will that work?

Some years ago, in Pontypool, South Wales, a manufacturing company used the kind of silver paper used in cigarette packets. It came on giant rolls which were taken off the line when low and sent to land-fill in skips. The Local Authority environmental officers identified another company locally, that also used this kind of silver paper, but in smaller quantities. So now the big rolls could become a by-product that could be sold on. It was worth an estimated £100k per year but the big company refused to get involved, saying it was too complicated and they just wanted to get on with their job.

Our manufacturing cycle now has reached the point in the cycle where we have to consider how the customers are going to be attracted. The best product in the world will be no good if no one knows it is there. The style and costs of marketing and all that goes with it, alter when the goods get bigger and more involved.

A leaflet was going around that looked like a hand-written compliments slip. It was for a business clearing gutters and doing similar work. Because it was hand-written people assumed it was local and it carried the feel of a young lad just going out to do something for himself. Admirable stuff and very clever.

However, word got around quickly, and some investigations showed these leaflets were going out across England and Wales. Not only was the company not locally based (the phone numbers were always mobile numbers) but they often did not turn up, and when they did, the job done was less than ideal. This was a cowboy firm who largely failed to satisfy their customer base. Some people paid out hundreds of pounds for roof cleaning or other work which was either dismal or non-existent. The firm's reputation online was in shreds, even if it had not been before the latest round of work.

Recruitment

Employing someone else does not mean twice the work done. Take someone on as your second person and you can reckon on one and half times the output. The reason is easy to see. Once the initial training and settling into the role has occurred then you can both get on with the work. However, someone has to look after the back-room office. Someone has to do all the promotion and other work to get business. It will all take a little longer now there are two of you.

Don't forget that the second person needs to produce (or allow to be produced) about three times their salary for it to be viable. Before you engage a second person run it through your Cash Flow Forecast to see if you can actually afford to do so, or what needs to happen before you can. Presuming all that planning has been done you are ready to engage someone.

Getting the right person is always important but it is especially critical for a small business where it is impossible to carry someone who is not right. The first step is to be very clear in your own mind what you want the employee to do and then to think out what skills they need to be able to fulfil the role. The job description should be a summary of the job and the application form should ask about the skills needed. A focus on skills helps to eliminate any discrimination – if you have a shortlist of people with the right skills, you can then go on to find out more about the individuals in an interview.

You could use an HR company. There are many small local businesses offering this service. They will help ensure that everything is within the law and can help you with wording advertisements and contracts. There are many subtleties to this. It is illegal to discriminate so demands or questions cannot be raised on the grounds of age, marital or relationship status, children, religion, nationality, gender and disability. Any suggestion towards any of these, even casually in interview, can land you up in an Employment Tribunal. Discrimination can be direct, indirect or just by association. It can apply to an employee, but also to someone you have not employed.

It can apply when you are involved in any of these stages of employment:

- Hiring Staff
- Setting Terms and Conditions of employment
- Training staff
- Promoting staff
- Handling a disciplinary or Grievance
- Dismissing an employee

In any case, there are other rules and legislation you must obey when you have employees who have rights under law you must know. Don't get it wrong! A few minutes doing a search on the Internet will bring up enough rules, regulations, examples to make you wonder how anyone employs anyone else, ever! Employ an HR specialist to advise and help.

> Finding the right person to employ is critical. Have a proper process; focus on the skills you need and consider help from an HR person.

Once you have all that sorted out you should look to Health and Safety legislation which is a discipline often crossing over with employment legislation. As far as your business goes there is other law covering Contracts, Premises, Late payments, Companies and Directors and more. You need to spend some time getting acquainted with the working world requirements but don't panic! You need to have knowledge of the general principles which will enable you to get help.

Tribunals

This is a court that considers matter of employment. They can decide if a case for discrimination or other grievance is justified and can levy fines where a company is found to be liable. Fines can be very substantial so these matters should not be taken lightly. There is also legislation about whistle blowers and employees who have had a case decided and what happens when they return to work. Basically, it is illegal to hold that against them although how that works in all circumstances is a question.

- Have a business plan that works for you.
- Nothing ever goes to plan – don't panic.
- Have back-up plans.
  Try to anticipate minor and major disasters:
  Ask yourself, "What could go wrong?"
- Pick customers carefully and check them out.
- Manage success and growth carefully:
  Keep all the parts of your business working well.
- Growth might mean more people.
  Do recruitment properly:
  The wrong person can do a lot of damage.
- Protect against fraudsters.

STARTING SOMETHING WITH NOTHING

Chapter Eleven
Strategies for the Future

No business stands still. Things change and customers come and go. What worked last year may not work so well this year. It's an unfortunate thing. Once you are in a business, it's very hard to see it from the outside.

Many businesses rise to a level, carry on for a while and for many reasons go into a decline.

Here are some suggestions to keep your business going:

- Do a regular check to see what your business looks like from the outside – ask people. If you have staff, do a mystery shopper on them in some way.

- Keep your eye on training needs, including for yourself.

- Check regularly on your messaging – are you giving out the right impression? Answering the phone, leaving messages, other responses? Your networking message?

- Does the material you use to back up your business – packaging, communication, banners, shop fronts, business backdrop – look as fresh as it should? If it looks tired, change it. The expense will be outweighed by the benefit.

- Are you clearly "open for business," in physical terms or in virtual terms? Why would anyone engage with you?

- Quality of service: Are you doing what you should to be prompt, on time and up to standard?

- Can you improve the way you describe things or handle enquiries and complaints? Remember: The response should always be a positive one.

- If you have staff, are they happy? It may seem obvious but somebody felt it was necessary to research this a year or two ago and arrived at the amazing conclusion that a happy staff was conducive to a successful business!

- Are all your reviews and compliance issues up to date and actually being complied with?

- Where is this business going? Remember: No business stands still. Having a plan that is pragmatic and realistic gives it all a focus. It is a plan. It may need revising and reviewing so don't consider it a failure if it takes longer or needs revision.

- Is everything in the business in proportion? Does it all work together and for you, rather than working against you?

- Time is your biggest and most important resource in so many ways. Use it wisely!

We have set out to be a guide to business that is easy to read and useful in content. The subject of starting and running a business is huge but we did not want to write a textbook.

For our potential borrowers, hopefully you will find enough encouragement here to take responsible and measured steps to start out properly.

For our potential supporters, hopefully you will see that Purple Shoots is not trying to change the world as such but is trying to make it better.

For our general readers, hopefully you will find something of interest here which will encourage you to become one of the two categories above.

For our students in business, hopefully you will find some nuggets in here that widen your perspective and take you out of the normal business tramlines with more hope of being successful in the future.

STARTING SOMETHING WITH NOTHING

Appendix 1
Some Stories

Fabienne Wilkinson

Fabienne relocated back to South Wales to be a single mum with a baby, in a new town with no contacts.

She found herself changed from a busy lifestyle with her fiancé, nice house and good career to living on her own, with a young baby in rented accommodation and claiming benefits all in a new location! Plus, there were now stuck with debts and no employment!

She found a part-time job and two years on she started thinking about what she could do to give herself an interest, utilise a lifetime of skills, fulfil a passion of helping others and prove to herself that she was still useful and earn some money.

Fabienne looked at her CV with her successful legal career as a Legal Assistant, Legal Secretary, Personal Assistant, Legal PA and experience in customer service. She was studying CILEX, a professional legal course and was only one year away from qualifying as a lawyer. However, as a single mum, she knew that the working environment and atmosphere of that industry with early starts and late finishes was just not possible at this time.

So what could she do?

Utilising her unique skills and experience and full of enthusiasm and a passion to help others, she decided that self-employment was her best route to fulfil her requirements and create a job for herself. The idea of her business "FAB-VA" was born! Her plan to do all the jobs a sole trader and small business can't always do: cover phones, produce invoices/look after expenses, chase clients and suppliers, manage their diary, create and maintain databases of contacts, provide holiday cover for phones/emails etc., produce documents/proofread, look after the clients' social media and even be their travel coordinator to make bookings.

Her next challenge was how to fund the start-up costs to cover what she needed and that is when she found Purple Shoots online. She liked the fact that it was a charity and it fitted with her ethics and, despite lockdown, was able to chat to them on the telephone and discuss her plans in detail, explore actions to start the business and how it could grow. Purple Shoots, unlike her bank, were happy to support a brand-new start-up, with no self-employment experience and having no cash to get it started! With Purple Shoots support it enabled her to complete a professional virtual assistant course, the equipment she would need to make this a professional business, to produce marketing materials, create a website and fund the cost of some business networking as a potential avenue to find her clients.

So, www.fab-va.co.uk https://www.facebook.com/FabVA20/ was created and Fabienne started looking for business owners who needed extra hours in their day to avoid burnout and could instead outsource to her giving them the ability to then concentrate on their core objectives.

Six months on and, despite the challenging lockdown trading conditions, she had made good progress with finding clients – sole traders, small business owners, consultants, lawyers and even doctors. She has found her niche: a paralegal virtual assistant. With her ten years in the legal industry, she has been able to offer a variety of legal support to assist solicitors, lawyers, in-house legal teams and barristers. Since the pandemic, Fabienne has also been able to assist solicitors with maternity, holiday, sick leave and COVID cover.

She supports business and personal needs, thereby helping business owners improve their productivity, efficiency and save money.

And for those very busy clients she has found herself managing their personal life with a variety of organising and researching all those tasks that they do not have time to sort themselves!

She has found the work extremely interesting and gives her a challenge to her day. Being able to work in a multitude of industries for all different sorts of people is the benefit of her business and something she thrives on, giving her different people to interact with and to have worthwhile conversations with.

Ian Thomas – Sparkle Pro Caravan Cleaning

An unlikely success story: a business that sprung up in the leisure industry, in the middle of the Coronavirus pandemic.

When COVID-19 first hit, Ian was one of the first casualties of the economic slump. Just two months into a new job, he was laid off without furlough and left wondering how to survive the looming recession.

So, with plenty of thinking time during the first lockdown, he started weighing up options: what was he good at, what caught his interest and where could he make a difference?

He thought of caravans. He'd sold them in a previous job and loved being around the holiday industry, where he'd always enjoyed meeting new people. So, he looked into the market to see what caravan owners needed most.

Answer: professional cleaning.

It's a specialist role, because caravans have their own unique cleaning and maintenance needs. Surely, there'd be room for a knowledgeable firm with a passion for customer service.

It felt right, so Ian went ahead and set up the business: Sparkle Pro Caravan Cleaning.

All he needed was a small loan to get started. But at first, he had no joy. His regular bank wasn't lending and as a new business he didn't qualify for the latest government funding. It seemed hopeless until he was pointed in our direction.

We quickly approved a loan of £3,000 as a down payment on a logo-ed vehicle. Then, armed with tools and leaflets, he hit the caravan parks, using the sales skills he'd built up over the past two decades.

He went door to door and much to his surprise, demand was overwhelming.

He cleaned his first caravan in July 2020, just four months after losing his job. The money he made was reinvested to buy better tools and more marketing materials. He was on his way.

Within two months he'd cleaned over seventy five caravans and every single one rebooked for the next year. Soon he had pages of five-star reviews online. Word was spreading. He even took on temporary staff, promising sixteen hours a week with scope for full-time work.

As Ian recalls, "I didn't expect to be that busy that soon!"

Of course, it doesn't end there. Caravan cleaning is a seasonal industry, where demand peaks in the summer. So autumn brought a new challenge: How will the business survive when it all goes quiet and how will they get ready to exploit the next boom when the parks reopen?

So Ian began making new plans:

- How to stay in touch with his customers and generate referrals.
- How to diversify, by cleaning inside as well as out.
- And how to stay busy in the off-season, by deep-cleaning static accommodation like holiday chalets.

There are challenges ahead for Ian, as for any new business, but this goes to show what people can do, even when they start with nothing but passion and a strong idea. Ian is making incredible inroads at the most challenging time. And yet, without intervention, his business would never have made it off the ground.

"I'm so happy having my own business, knowing I've made that step to do something of my own. There's a long way to go, of course, but it's all going in the right direction. I'd recommend Purple Shoots to anyone who needs help getting started." www.sparkleprocaravancleaning.co.uk

Jane Mullins

After a period of her children's illnesses, spouse job losses and her own ill-health, which had left the whole family at a very low point financially, Jane wanted to start again and rebuild her career and her family's circumstances. She had previously worked in dementia care and seen examples of poor uninformed practice, but also some really excellent care which has inspired what she has done since. She wanted to establish a training company which would teach people how to care for people living with dementia well while also learning to care for themselves to become resilient, well care workers. Because she hadn't been working for a couple of years and had no funds to put in, no one would support her until she met Purple Shoots. After that first meeting, she said she could see a chink of light beginning to shine at the end of the long dark tunnel she'd been in.

With the loan she established her business DUETcare and it took off – training people from the public and private sector and becoming recognised as an expert in her field. As a result, she was encouraged to write a book and this has been published with the help of another small loan from Purple Shoots. The book is called "Finding the Light in Dementia" and is aimed at families and individuals caring for loved ones living with dementia; a simple and practical guide to help families and friends know what to say and do when caring for their loved ones living with the condition. It's a great book – everyone should have a copy – and it is a testament to her courage, perseverance and determination and her passion for caring for people living with dementia. You can buy her book on Amazon:

https://www.findingthelightindementia.com/

Since the Covid lockdown, she has been acutely aware of the many issues exacerbated by the enforced isolation for people living with dementia and their families and for the stress and challenges presented to care staff and providers. She has devised a plan to take **DUETcare**™ online, offering affordable dementia training and staff wellbeing resources to help all affected. For health and social care staff it will provide excellent care and support and for the care providers, it will address many of the challenges of staff retention. **DUETcare**™ will also provide fantastic activities to help family carers communicate and stay connected with their loved ones living with dementia.

Jordan Jones – RiKaSysTemZ Ltd

Jordan started her career as a Zumba and later a fitness instructor and when we met her, she had already been running her business for five years.

RiKaSysTemZ is a fitness and nutrition business, but it is also about encouraging emotional and psychological well-being through offering friendly, non-threatening sessions and providing advice and help with accompanying nutritional education. Jordan herself had been through difficult times in the past which had sapped her confidence and so has a deep understanding of, and empathy with, her member base.

When the business started, it was from rented premises, but the costs were very high and she struggled to sustain the business effectively. She experimented with some different models but now has one which works. She trains instructors for free and provides them with equipment, access to her routines etc. Thereafter, the instructor pays her a proportion of takings as he/she develops classes. There are systems in place to ensure quality of delivery is maintained.

The loan was to help her grow and to seize opportunities which she was creating by going into schools and expanding her network of instructors. There is now a network of instructors across the UK and a strong brand developing – RiKaShaKe® is a mini trampoline fitness workout and there are another eleven different RiKa class formats to keep her members engaged and progressing. The Klub is all about nutrition and provides an in-depth understanding of nutrition to accompany the physical aspect.

The loan, inadvertently, also prepared Jordan and the business for the introduction of the lockdowns. Part of the loan was invested into improving the online presence and as a result of the lockdown hitting, Jordan was able to take the whole business online and all of the members were able to continue with classes throughout the entire lockdown period.

Julie Hawkins

Julie approached Purple Shoots when she was based in Monmouth in 2018.

She had already spent a number of difficult years trying to build her business alongside being a single parent, completing a law degree and working part-time in low-paid roles. Julie had a strong career history before becoming a single parent in 2012 and the barriers to flexible work in-line with her skillset and pay scale meant a significant reduction in income, repossession of her property, high private rents and an adversely affected credit file. Not wanting to be forced into relative poverty due to being a primary carer, Julie continued to fight for her right to work within her skillset, to enhance her knowledge through law and to sustain and grow her business.

Julie had taken an initial loan with a charity in 2013 to launch her business before she had any sales, but it took a couple of years for her to truly understand her audience, by which time her marketing budget was all gone and her cost of living so high that she couldn't achieve the required level of exposure to the correct market. Her product is a pregnancy cushion that enables ladies to lay prone at variable stages of pregnancy, called a KIH Bed (see below URL). She invented it when she was expecting and named the product after her daughter. Her initial marketing budget was aimed at pregnant ladies, but following a couple of years of organic sales she understood that instead her market was professional practitioners (osteopaths, spa hotels, massage therapists, physio and chiropractors). Sadly, this was the point at which she could not obtain further lending to market to the correct audience when she actually had sales.

www.kihproducts.co.uk

With the frustration of not being able to secure part-time qualifying employment and being unable to find the budget on a low wage to pay for increased exposure for her business, Julie continued to work for low pay and continued to apply for some benefits and to use high-interest pay day loans to make up her rent shortfall. Julie ran a Facebook campaign to ask for legal work in school hours and this paid off. She has been working freelance as a Paralegal for two years from home. Julie also carried out some freelance business development work for another company. Julie wanted to pour all her lessons learned from being a single mum in to helping others and launched the Single Mums Business Network (SMBN).

www.singlemumsbusinessnetwork.com

This was when she was able to ask Purple Shoots for a loan. She knew that she could repay in any event from all the activities, even if the business side didn't pick up quickly. The money was used to exhibit her KIH products at the NEC in Birmingham and promote the SMBN. She was able to demonstrate the KIH bed, discuss with interested parties for both KIH & SMBN and even took a Purple Shoots banner to advertise there!

This exposure, to the correct market, turned her business around and enabled her to truly identify what was holding her back. None of the high street lenders would help Julie, due to her adverse credit rating and, had it not been for Purple Shoots, Julie would still be working in an under-skilled role, for low pay and likely still struggling to pay creditors with a long-term need for benefits. Instead, because she was given some humane trust, she is financially independent.

She now campaigns, via the Single Mums Business Network, for Government to recognise that it is the barriers to salaried work and finance that trap people in a long-term cycle of benefits. Through the SMBN she helps her members gain affordable exposure, so that they do not struggle for as long as she did.

Her company now supports five other UK manufacturers, a self-employed seamstress and a freelance executive assistant.

Julie supports Gingerbread charity with a five per cent contribution of SMBN member fees and Julie repaid her loan in full to Purple Shoots, eighteen months early.

Katie Davies

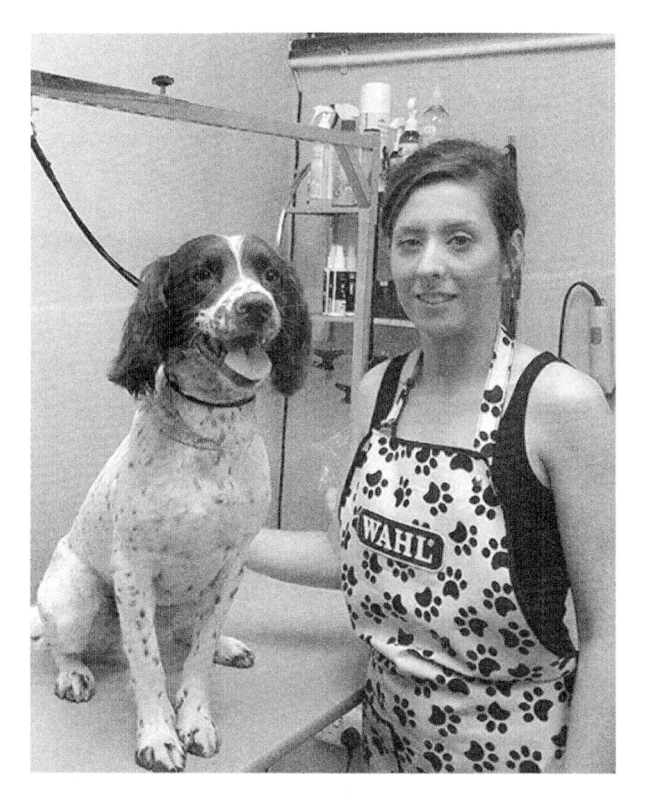

Katie has a great rapport and skill with dogs and her ambition was to be a dog groomer. She followed a basic course at college but realised whilst working in a dog grooming salon that this hadn't equipped her fully to be able to offer a good service to all types and ages of dogs; nor to run her own business. She cast around for more courses and found a good one but she didn't have the funds to pay for it and couldn't find a lender prepared to support her so that she could reach her goal. Purple

Shoots offered her a small loan which was enough to pay for the course and to get some additional equipment.

Having completed the course, she started her business in a shared space and began to develop a regular client base. She has now moved into her own premises which she revised, redecorated and kitted out as a perfect place for dogs to be groomed.

"Pretty Little Paws" is in the Fairwater shops in Cwmbran, with easy parking and a welcoming place which gives dogs and their owners the best possible experience. She is building her regular customers – dogs of all sizes, breeds and ages – and is now looking at adding extra services as the business develops (such as dental care and a dog jacuzzi for elderly dogs and dogs with arthritis). As the business continues to grow, she hopes to take on another groomer.

Ruth Hancock

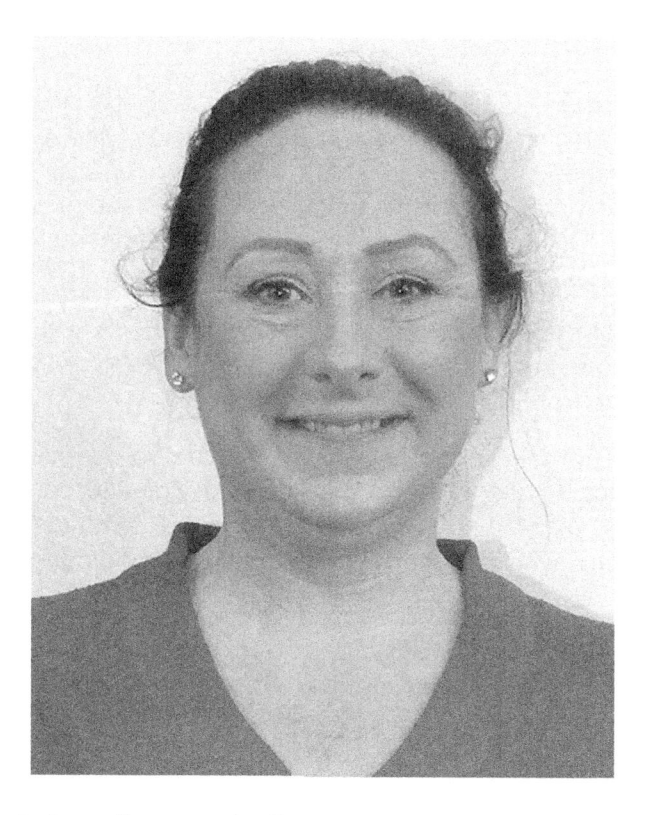

Ruth is from Rumney in Cardiff and was a working mum until a serious bout of anxiety coupled with OCD meant that she had to give up work. As she was recovering, she decided that she wanted to start working again but in a way which would accommodate her illness and allow her to be at home.

She is artistic and is passionate about the need for "green" products, so she channelled this into developing a range of artisan soaps which are vegan as well as "green," – some of them in beautiful designs and colours as gift soaps.

The designs are all her own, making clever use of moulds and her own work. She got the necessary licences but knew that she needed some funding to enable her to create a proper manufacturing space (in a summerhouse in her garden) and to get some more equipment so she could manufacture on a larger scale.

Her time out of work had left her with a poor credit score and low confidence – exacerbated by failing to get funding from other providers.

Purple Shoots supported her (we could see no reason for her not to be confident). She had considered every aspect of starting a business and her products were beautiful, with five-star ratings on her Facebook page.

She is now getting bespoke orders from groups and companies for specially designed soaps as well as a growing customer base for her plain and gift soaps.

Her products have expanded to wax melts, bath bombs and other novelties.

The business is called Bwthyn.Y ou can buy her products through the below URL.

https://bwthyn.co.uk/

Appendix 2
Cashflow Template

Cashflow Forecast

	Jan	to	Dec
Business Income			
Sales Income			
Cost of Sales (Stock)			
Purple Shoots loan			
Grant			
Wages (partner) and benefits			
Benefits			
Gross Net Income (A) (income after cost of sales)	0	0	0
Business Costs			
Owner's Drawings (pay)			
Wages of any employees			
Rent Rates & Water (business)			
Accountancy (Quickbooks fee)			
Insurances (business)			
Web Site Costs			
Light & Heat (business)			
Bank Charges & Interest			
Internet			
Repairs & Maintenance			
Printing Postage & Stationery			
Advertising			
Telephone			
Computer Running Costs			
Car tax, insurance, MOT			
Motor Running Costs (Fuel, repairs)			
Loan Repayments to Purple Shoots			
Other loan repayments			
Capital Expenditure (buying equipment, vehicles etc)			
Credit Card Processing Charges			
Other Expenses			
Home Costs			
Total costs from Personal Budget			
Taxes			
Total Costs (B)	0	0	0
Difference between income and costs (A) - (B)	0	0	0
Money left taken to next month		0	0
Money left in the business	0	0	0

BOB SHEPHERD & KAREN DAVIES

About the Authors

We are Bob and Karen and we have spent many years looking at small businesses and seeing how they work.

Karen had the idea for Purple Shoots from organisations in far-flung places around the world delivering micro-loans and changing lives with them. She saw many people in the UK with good ideas and the ability to see them through, but without enough money to get them started. Therefore, she started Purple Shoots alongside Bob in order to specifically support such people.

Purple Shoots has grown from a small beginning in Wales to the only organisation in the UK helping people off the ground with a small business loan when they have been dealt a bad hand in life and can't find anyone to believe in them. We also run self-determined groups, the Purple Shoots Greenhouse and other things which create pathways for the most left-behind people to move forward into something enterprising.

How do we do it? Certainly not by basing it on rigid formulae. Basically, if you have a valid business idea and a bit of "oomph," Purple Shoots would like to help.

So, play with the ideas in this book, put them into practice, get out there and do it.

https://purpleshoots.org

About PublishU

PublishU is transforming the world of publishing.

PublishU has developed a new and unique approach to publishing books, offering a three-step guided journey to becoming a globally published author!

We enable hundreds of people a year to write their book within 100-days, publish their book in 100-days and launch their book over 100-days to impact tens of thousands of people worldwide.

The journey is transformative, one author said,
"I never thought I would be able to write a book, let alone in 100 days... now I'm asking myself what else have I told myself that can't be done that actually can?'"

To find out more visit
www.PublishU.com

Printed in Great Britain
by Amazon